monday morning®

Patterns for U.S. History

written and illustrated by Marilynn G. Barr

W9-ABY-705

Publisher: Roberta Suid
Copy Editor: Carol Whiteley
Production: MGB Press

For a complete catalog, please write to the address below:
P.O. Box 1680, Palo Alto, CA 94302

ISBN 1-878279-93-9

Printed in the United States of America

987654321

TABLE OF CONTENTS

Introduction

Take your students on a journey through American history, from the first Americans to the early settlers to Colonial America to the Revolution and the age of invention with *Patterns for U.S. History.*

Patterns for U.S. History includes maps and patterns for a dwelling, people, foods, tools, animals, transportation devices, communication equipment, inventions, and landmarks for ten different periods of American history. Pattern pages include basic information about home life, industry, natural resources, geography, and historical events.

Your students will also enjoy making their own crafts, such as Colonial hornbooks and patchwork autobiographies. Literature Links will introduce students to featured books about each historical period.

How to Use the Patterns

- The actual patterns can be used to create dioramas, collages, mobiles, and hand puppets. They can also be used as visuals for student reports.
- Patterns can be enlarged for bulletin board displays or puppet theater productions.
- Students can use the patterns as templates or as references to create their own images.

For Dioramas

Provide students with the materials listed below to create dramatic dioramas.

- corrugated board — a large sheet can be used as a platform
- spools — attach to backs to make free-standing patterns
- crepe paper — to decorate the inside or outside of the shoe box
- old silk flowers — for landscapes or decorating
- Popsicle sticks — to use as wooden beams, flooring, fencing, or roofing
- aluminum foil — for roofing, windows, or jewelry
- plastic wrap — for windows or to create the illusion of water
- bark mulch — for landscapes or painted to resemble rocks
- pine straw — for roofing or to make hay or wheat stacks
- craft tissue — to create flames
- cotton balls — to create clouds or cotton fields
- scrap cloth — for woven cloth props or to attach to patterns
- clay — to make pottery and sculptures
- brown grocery bags — to use for stucco or mud-brick buildings
- large buttons — can be used as plates and serving pieces
- pipe cleaners — can be formed into tools, necklaces, and other props

For Collages

Students can use the patterns to create colorful collages showing a variety of items from one culture.

For instance, to make a cultural collage, provide students with enlarged maps of the Lewis and Clark Expedition. Have students color, cut out, and glue the maps to a sheet of poster board.

Then provide students with the patterns for the Western Frontier. Also provide magazines for additional cut-out pictures, and a variety of craft supplies for students to complete their Lewis and Clark Expedition Collage.

For Hand Puppets

The people and animal patterns can be used to make hand puppets. Have children color and cut out the patterns.

To make hand puppets using Popsicle sticks, have children apply glue to one end of a stick and attach it to the back of a pattern.

To make hand puppets using paper bags, have children apply glue to the backs of patterns and attach each one to a separate bag.

To make hand puppets using old gloves or mittens, have children apply glue to the back of a pattern and attach it to the palm side of an old glove or mitten.

For Book Report Visuals

Show students how to create book report visuals. Provide children with construction paper, crayons, scissors, glue, and patterns for a book report on a specific historical period.

Demonstrate how to cut various size and shape frames from construction paper. Then show how to use the frames to highlight patterns, drawings, or cutouts used as visuals.

For Bulletin Board Displays

Enlarge patterns to display on your bulletin board. For a 3-D effect, attach various size box lids to the backs of patterns before mounting on the board.

Trace and cut clothing for people from wallpaper or cloth scraps. Add buttons, feathers, and other craft materials.

For a student work display board, reproduce a dwelling pattern for each student to color and cut out. Provide a sheet of construction paper, crayons, scissors, and glue.

Show students how to fold construction paper for a booklet cover. They can glue the cut-out dwelling on the front. Attach booklet covers to the board.

Trace the outline of the same dwelling pattern on white paper for students to practice writing and other class work. Have students insert completed assignments in their dwelling booklets.

For Puppet Theater Productions

Enlarge patterns to make a puppet theater using the bulletin board as the background and a large cardboard box on a table as the working theater.

Decorate your bulletin board with patterns from one of the historical periods in this book. Position a table in front of the bulletin board decorated with matching terrain. Cover and cut a window in a large cardboard box to look like a dwelling on the board. For a brick structure, cover the box with brown paper bags. Use crumpled white construction paper for stucco. Use hay, straw, or green construction paper for thatched dwellings.

Provide students with patterns to color and cut out to make puppets and props.

Then help students prepare a script and perform a play about the people of the community entitled "A Day in the Life of a ___." Invite parents to attend the performance.

As Templates

Students can use the patterns in this book as resources to create their own drawings or patterns. They can also use the actual patterns (cut out and colored) to make mobiles, greeting cards, or to paste in scrapbooks. Students can also use the patterns as templates to create outline drawings, which they can decorate themselves.

Show students how to trace around cut-out patterns. Then show how to add features and other details.

For Mobiles

Provide students with hangers, paper plates, or corrugated board to form a mobile base.

Once children have colored and cut out patterns, show how to punch a hole in each pattern. Tie yarn to patterns and attach loose ends to the mobile base. Hang finished mobiles from your classroom ceiling.

For Scrapbooks

Provide students with oak tag, colored construction paper pages, crayons, scissors, and glue to make scrapbooks.

Have each child make and decorate a scrapbook cover. Punch two holes along the left side of the cover and scrapbook pages. Insert construction paper pages between the book covers. Lace and tie a length of yarn or ribbon through the holes of the scrapbook.

For Greetings and Posters

Provide students with construction paper, poster board, crayons, scissors, glue, and patterns to make greeting cards or posters.

The First Americans (1550-1600)
Native American Territories

The first Americans came from Asia more than 20,000 years ago. Many small groups settled across what is now North America in the nine cultural regions shown below.

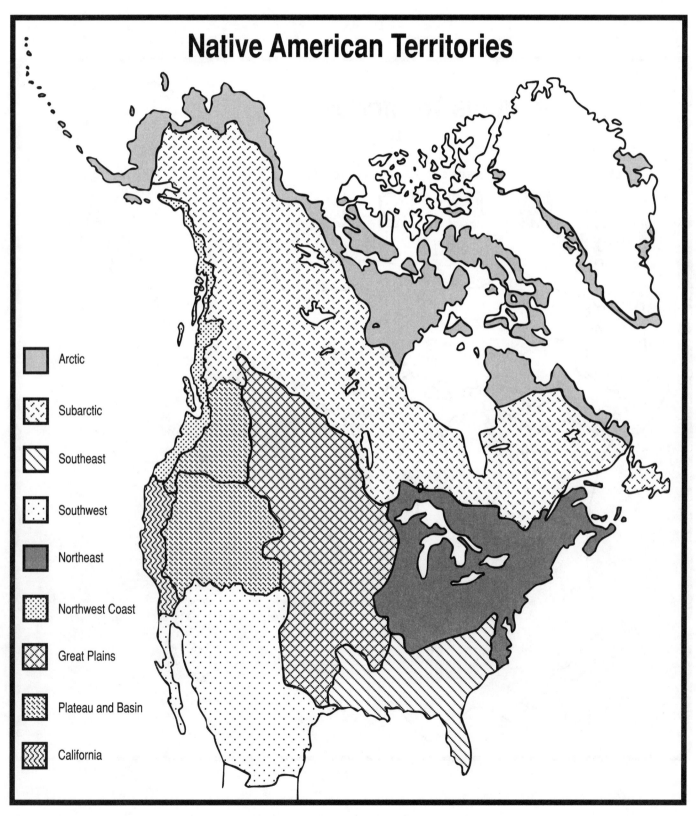

Native American Territories

Legend:
- Arctic
- Subarctic
- Southeast
- Southwest
- Northeast
- Northwest Coast
- Great Plains
- Plateau and Basin
- California

Northeastern Native Americans

Iroquois Territories

The Iroquois people, who consist of the Seneca, Cayuga, Onondaga, Oneida, and Mohawk tribes, settled in areas known today as Ohio, Pennsylvania, New York, Vermont, and portions of Ontario, Canada.

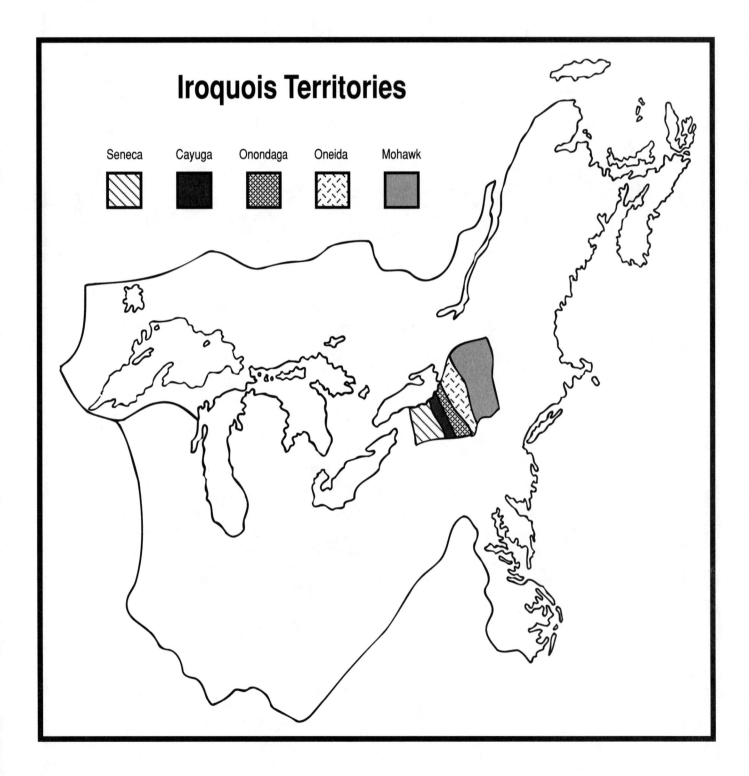

Bulletin Board: An Iroquois Community

1. Enlarge the patterns on pages 12-18.
2. Color and cut out the patterns.
3. Cover your bulletin board with brown paper for the ground and blue paper for the sky.
4. Cut 6" widths of brown craft paper for stockade planks and attach two on either side of the bulletin board.
5. Add a brown bulletin board border.
6. Enlarge, color, and cut out the title below.
7. Arrange and attach the patterns to your bulletin board.

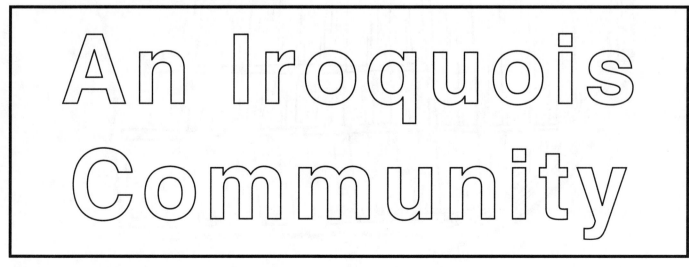

Bulletin Board Patterns: An Iroquois Dwelling

Iroquois families lived in stockades with several "long houses." A long house was a structure made of bark and wood. Each was divided into several apartments with a door on each end. An average long house measured 25 feet by 80 feet. The largest measured 25 feet by 200 feet and housed up to 20 families.

Bulletin Board Patterns:
Animals of an Iroquois Community

Animals found in Iroquois territories included deer, wolves, foxes, beavers, and a variety of turtles. A variety of birds, such as grouse and turkey, and fish, such as salmon and trout, were also seen. Freshwater clams were also found in Iroquois territories, a favorite food item.

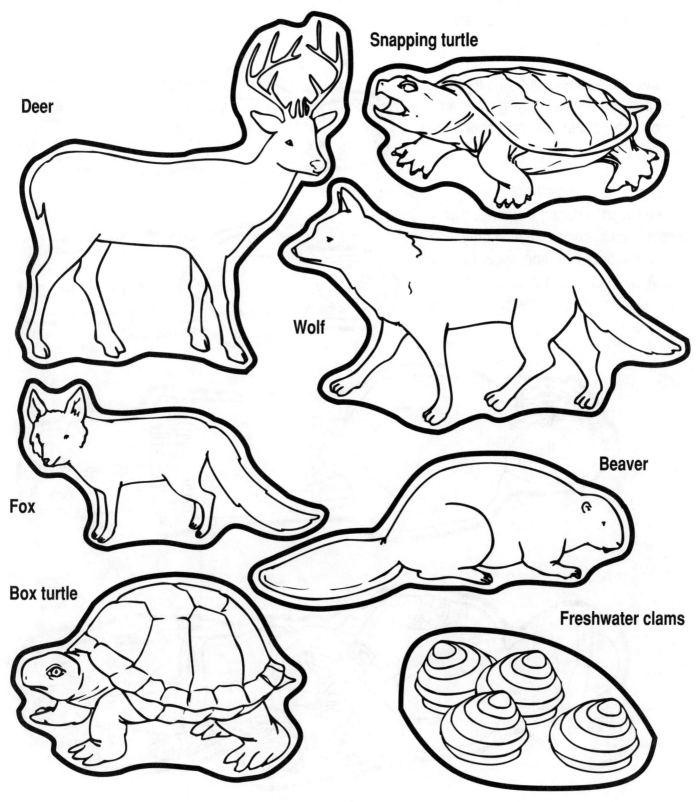

Deer

Snapping turtle

Wolf

Fox

Beaver

Box turtle

Freshwater clams

Bulletin Board Patterns:
People of an Iroquois Community

Before the arrival of Europeans, the Iroquois wore clothing made from buckskin. Clothing was often decorated with porcupine quills, moose hair, and other natural items.

After the Europeans' arrival, the Iroquois made traditional-style clothing of woven cloth decorated with buttons, ribbons, and beads.

Men wore kilts or breechcloths and beaded leggings during warm weather months. During colder weather they also wore shirts, buckskin moccasins, furs, and caps. A cap looked like a derby with feathers attached to the back.

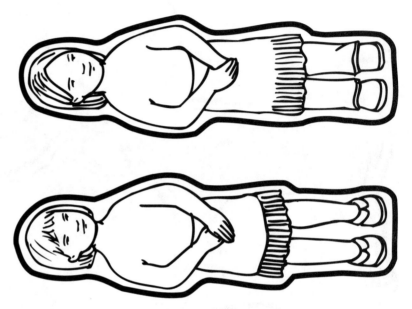

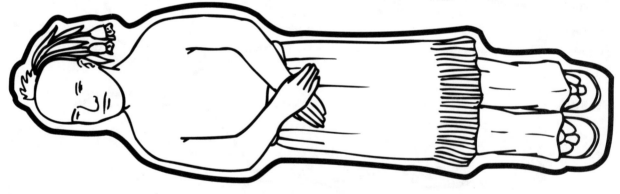

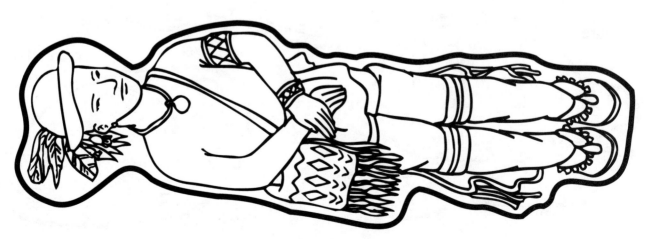

Bulletin Board Patterns:
People of an Iroquois Community

Iroquois women wore buckskin skirts, leggings, and woven cornhusk slippers during the summer months. During the winter they wore dresses, buckskin moccasins, and furs.

More Patterns for Native America
Food, Tools, Footwear, and Weapons

The Iroquois, once hunters and gatherers, developed into a successful farming culture. Their main crop was corn. They also grew a variety of beans and squashes. Tobacco was grown for a variety of uses.

All meals included some form of corn cooked in pottery and wooden cookware. Other food items such as nuts, fish, and meat were also part of the Iroquois diet.

1. **Baskets** were used for harvested crops, as sieves for ground corn, and for drying berries and corn.
2. **Deer jawbones** were used for scraping corn off a cob.
3. **Wooden bowls** were used for serving bread.
4. **Rakes** or **plows** were used for farming crops.
5. **Bows and arrows** were the main hunting weapons.
6. **Cradle boards** were decorated with carvings.
7. **Snowshoes** were made from hickory frames and deerskin webbing and looked much like modern snowshoes.
8. **Buckskin moccasins** were decorated with beads.

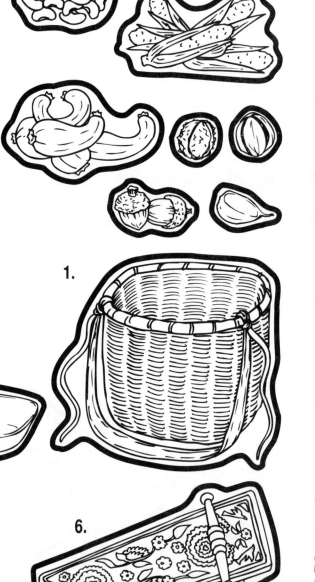

1.

2.

3.

4.

5.

6.

7.

8.

More Patterns for Native America
Jewelry, Instruments, and Transportation

The Iroquois made everything they needed from natural materials. Pottery was usually formed around gourds. During firing the gourd burned away leaving a rounded bottom pot.

1. **Snapping turtle rattles** were used by members of the False Face Society during special ceremonies.
2. **Gourd rattles** were used to accompany singers.
3. **Box turtle rattles** were used for the Woman's Dance.
4. **Cowhorn rattles** were used by singers and dancers.
5. **Axe heads** were chiseled from stones.
6. **Canoes** were made from elm and hickory trees.
7. **Combs** were carved from animal bones.
8. **Broaches** were made from silver and displayed traditional Iroquois symbols.

Gourd pottery

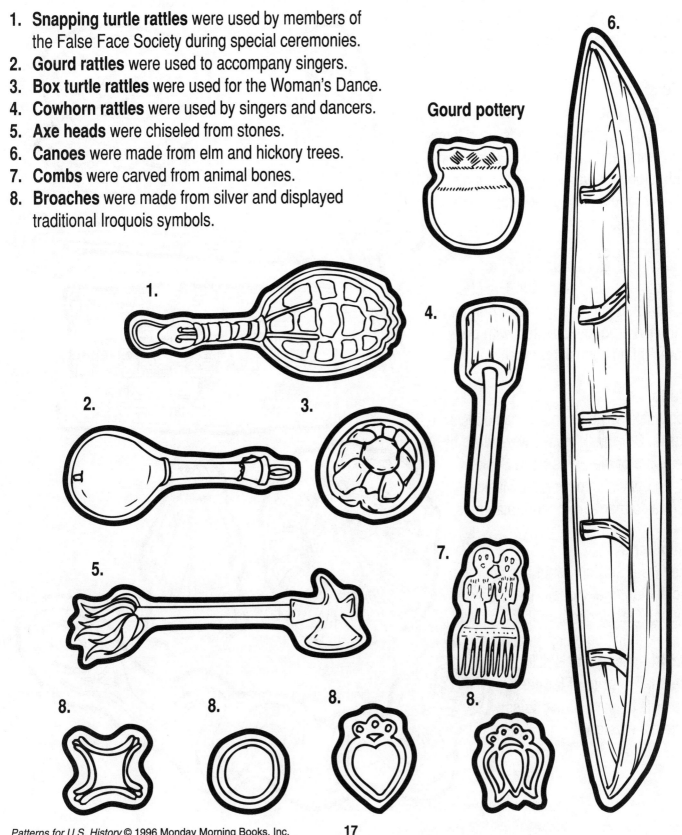

More Patterns for Native America
Games, Valuables, Crafts, and Landmarks

Games

The Iroquois played a variety of games. Lacrosse, a popular game, was played in much the same way as it is today. A game of chance consisted of a decorated bowl filled with six peach pits charred on one side. A player would rap the bowl on the ground. If five pits of the same color showed face up, the player would score and take another turn. If not, the next player would take a turn.

Valuables

Wampum, decorative beadwork, was a valuable trading gift. Traditional beads were formed from white and purple shells. Europeans understood the value of wampum and began manufacturing it for trade with the Iroquois.

A notched staff was used by the Iroquois sachem, or leader. The staff was divided into five sections, one for each of the five Iroquois cultures, with pegs representing council members.

Crafts

Cornhusks were used to make dolls and masks. Cornhusk masks were worn by members of the False Face Society during special ceremonies. Masks were also made from other materials.

Landmarks

The Great Serpent Mound is an ancient landmark located in Adams County, Ohio, once Iroquois territory. This earthen sculpture measures 1,254 feet long and is still 5 feet tall in spite of farmers' attempts to level it. Its origins remain a mystery.

Native American Craft Activities

Let's Make an Iroquois Diorama

Ask each student to bring an empty shoe box to school. Provide paint and brushes for students to paint their boxes to resemble an Iroquois region.

Reproduce the patterns on pages 12-18 for students to color, cut out, and glue inside their dioramas.

When dioramas are completed, display student projects on a table in front of your Iroquois Community bulletin board.

Let's Make Moccasin Shoe Covers

Provide students with construction paper, scissors, markers, paint, brushes, beans, rice, glue, a hole punch, and a 20" length of yarn to make beaded moccasin shoe covers. Have children cut two 4" x 5" pieces of construction paper for the top of their moccasins as shown. Also cut two 4" x 12" strips for the ankle bands.

Encourage children to decorate their ankle bands and tops using beans, rice, markers, and paint. Show how to cut a fringed edge along one side of each ankle band. Then punch holes as shown on each band and moccasin top. To assemble the pieces: hold the band face up and lace a length of yarn through the first hole on the right side. Then lace the yarn through the hole on the left side of the moccasin top as shown. Continue lacing around the top of the band. At the last hole, lace the yarn through the moccasin top, then through the band.

Native American Literature Links

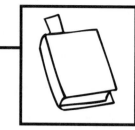

Indian Signs and Signals
by George Frovnal
Bonanza Books, 1979

Learn about different forms of American Indian communication including sign language, smoke and trail signals, and more.

Sign Language Slogans

Invite children to write slogans in sign language to display on a communications bulletin board. Provide torn grocery bag sheets to resemble leather or bark on which children may paint their slogans. Have children crumple, then smooth the sheets before painting.

| Man | Woman | Tree | Buffalo | Deer | Horse | Sun | Rain |

More Books About the First Americans

Brother Eagle, Sister Sky
by Susan Jeffers, Dial Books, 1991

Buffalo Hunt
by Russell Freedman, Holiday House, 1988

Buffalo Woman
by Paul Goble, Bradbury Press, 1984

Crow Chief
by Paul Goble, Orchard Books, 1992

The First Americans
by Joy Hakim, Oxford University Press, 1993

The Gift of the Sacred Dog
by Paul Goble, Bradbury Press, 1980

The Girl Who Loved Wild Horses
by Paul Goble, Bradbury Press, 1978

Hiawatha
by Henry Wadsworth Longfellow, Dial Books, 1983

Hiawatha and the Iroquois League
by Megan McClard, Silver Burdette Press, 1989

Hiawatha's Childhood
by Henry Wadsworth Longfellow, Farrar,
Straus & Giroux, 1984

Hiawatha: Messenger of Peace
by Dennis B. Fradin, McElderry Books, 1992

The Indian in the Cupboard
by Banks Reid, Doubleday, 1980

Island of the Blue Dolphins
by Scott O'Dell, Houghton Mifflin, 1990

Knots on a Counting Rope
by Bill Martin, Holt & Company, 1987

Powwow
by George Ancona, Harcourt Brace Jovanovich, 1993

Raven
by Gerald McDermott, Harcourt Brace Jovanovich, 1993

Sky Dogs
by Jane Yolen, Harcourt Brace Jovanovich, 1990

The Story of Jumping Mouse
by John Steptoe, Lothrop, Lee & Shepard, 1984

Totem Pole
by Diane Holt-Goldsmith, Holiday House, 1990

When Clay Sings
by Byrd Baylor, Scribner's, 1972

Early American Settlements (1600-1650)
Early Dutch and English Settlements

In the early 1600s, Europeans began to cross the Atlantic Ocean seeking fortunes and freedom. The English and Dutch were the first Europeans to settle in the New World.

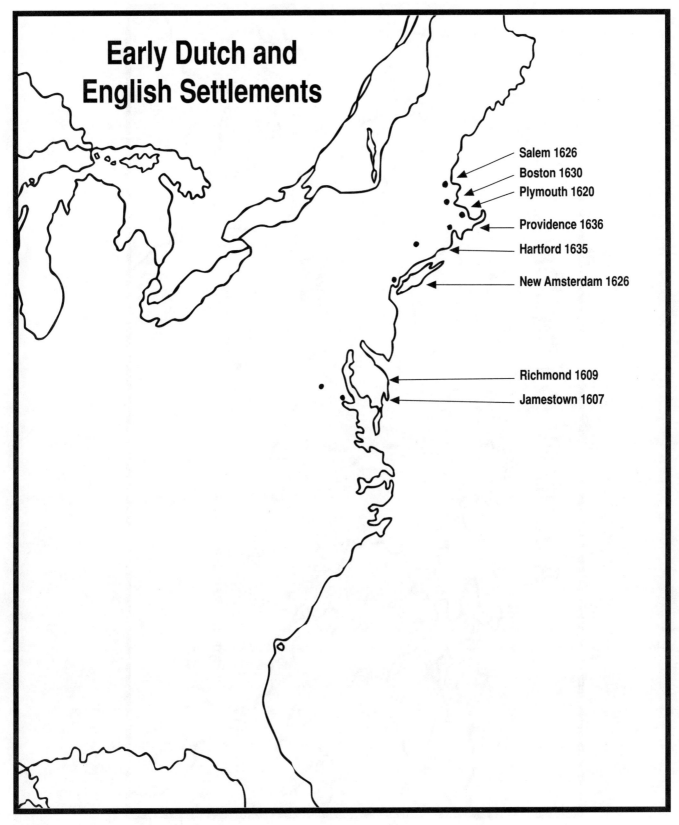

Early Dutch and English Settlements

Salem 1626
Boston 1630
Plymouth 1620
Providence 1636
Hartford 1635
New Amsterdam 1626
Richmond 1609
Jamestown 1607

Early American Settlements (1600-1650)
The Plymouth Colony

In September 1620, a group of English people called Pilgrims sailed across the Atlantic Ocean in a tiny ship called the *Mayflower*. On December 21, 1620, they arrived in Cape Cod Bay, known today as Massachusetts, and established the Plymouth Colony settlement.

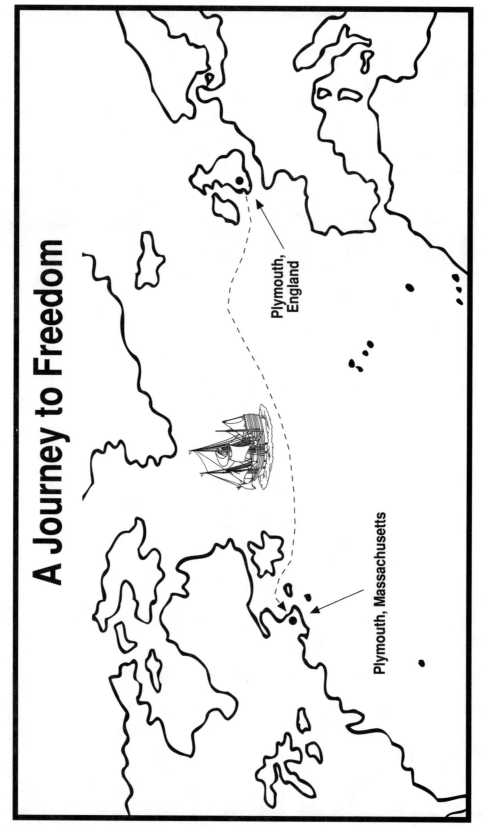

A Journey to Freedom

Plymouth, England

Plymouth, Massachusetts

Bulletin Board: A Plymouth Community

1. Enlarge the patterns on pages 24-30.
2. Color and cut out the patterns.
3. Cover your bulletin board with brown paper for the ground and blue paper for the sky.
4. Add an orange bulletin board border.
5. Enlarge, color, and cut out the title below.
6. Arrange and attach the patterns to your bulletin board.

Bulletin Board Patterns: A Plymouth Colony Dwelling

Early settlers lived in structures built from logs and covered with clay to keep out the rain and cold.

Bulletin Board Patterns:
Animals of the Plymouth Colony

Animals found in and around the Plymouth settlement included deer, geese, ducks, wild turkeys, pigeons, and quail. A variety of fish, lobster, oysters, and clams were also seen.

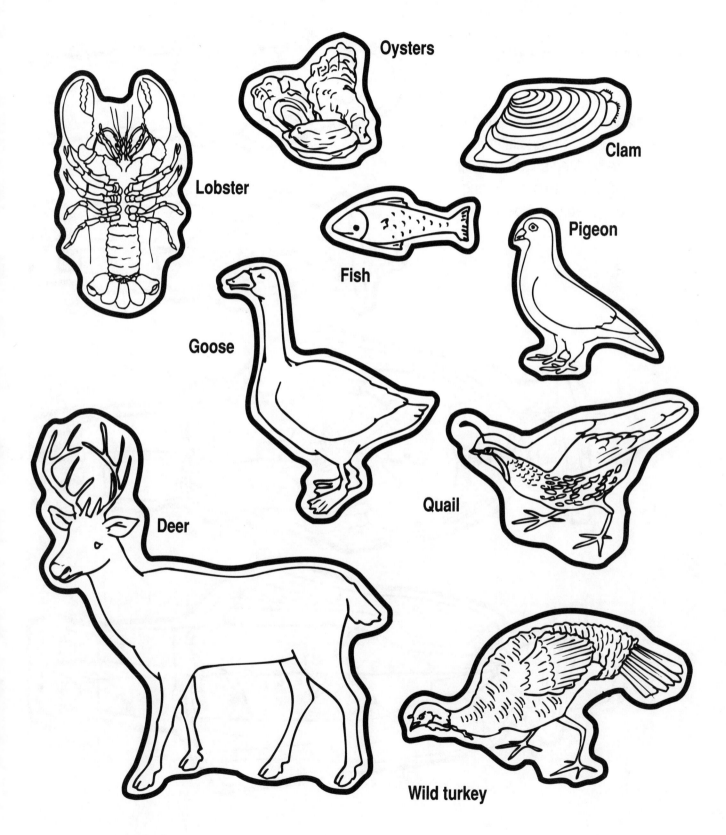

Oysters

Clam

Lobster

Fish

Pigeon

Goose

Quail

Deer

Wild turkey

Bulletin Board Patterns:
People of the Plymouth Colony

Early settlers wore plain yet useful clothing. Most garments were made from homespun cloth dyed with leaves and berries. Garments were mended, cut, and reused.

A Pilgrim man wore a tall brimmed hat, tight knee breeches, a wide-collared shirt, stockings, wide buckled shoes, and either a vest or a long buttoned coat. During colder weather he wore a cape.

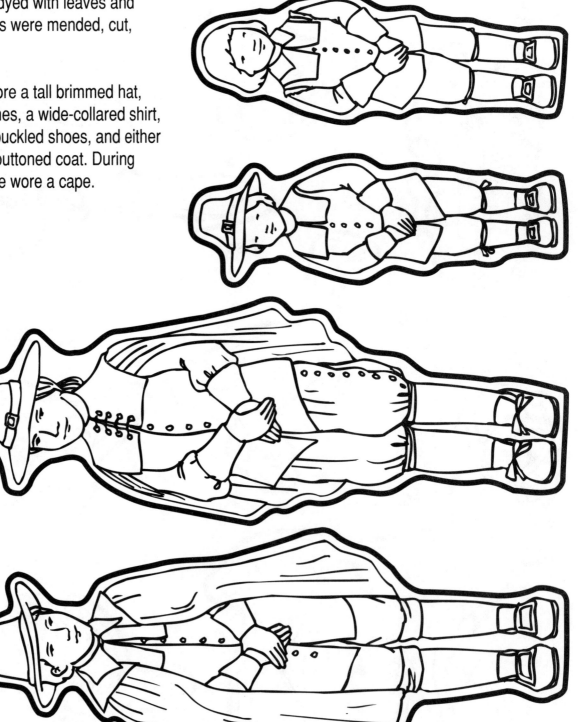

Bulletin Board Patterns:
People of the Plymouth Colony

Pilgrim women dressed in plain dark-colored dresses and aprons, and wore caps to cover their heads. They also wore capes during colder weather.

More Patterns for the Plymouth Colony
Food, Utensils, and Celebrations

Corn was the early settler's most important food. Native Americans taught the early settlers how to use it. The early settlers also raised carrots, turnips, pumpkins, squash, potatoes, and a variety of berries.

The first Thanksgiving was celebrated in December of 1621. The settlers shared the celebration with the Native Americans, giving thanks for their first successful harvest. A feast of turkey, deer, goose, duck, fish, cornmeal bread, succotash, nuts, and pumpkin stewed in maple sap was served over the three-day celebration.

1. **Iron kettles** were used to prepare food over an open log fire.
2. **Pies** were filled with berries.
3. **Cooking utensils** were made of wood.
4. **Porringers**, wooden containers with a handle, were used as bowls.
5. **Mortars and pestles** were used to grind foods.

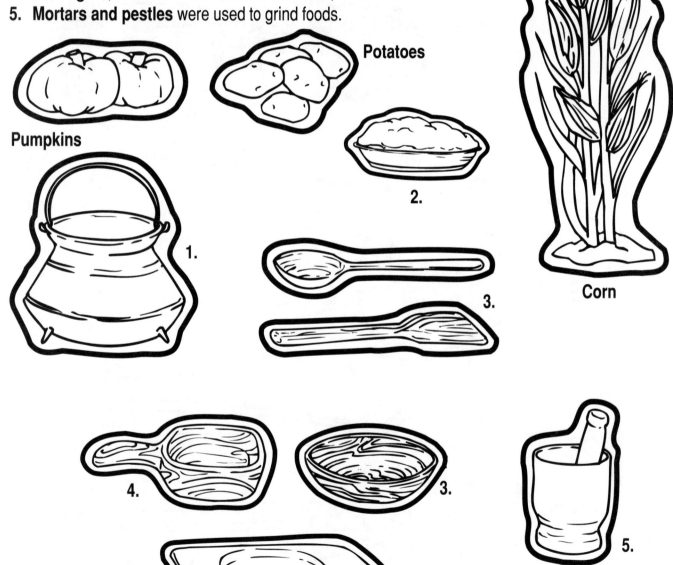

Potatoes

Pumpkins

1.

2.

3.

Corn

4.

3.

3.

5.

More Patterns for the Plymouth Colony
Tools and Transportation

Trees were one of the most important resources for the early settler. Settlers used the wood from trees to build shelters and to make almost every device, tool, and utensil necessary for living in the New World.

Early roads were few and rough to travel, so many early settlers used rafts and dugout canoes to travel by water.

1. **Sickles** were used to clear brush and harvest crops.
2. **Barrels** were used to store food or liquid.
3. **Canteens**, round containers with carrying straps, held liquids.
4. **Brooms** were made of wood and straw.
5. **Dugout canoes** were rough carved from tree trunks.

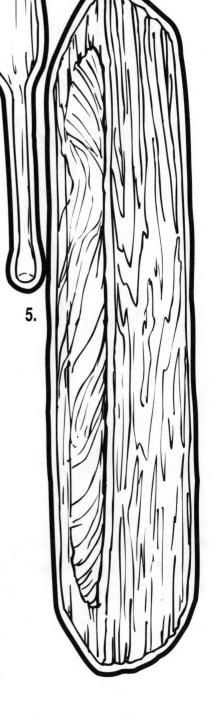

More Patterns for the Plymouth Colony
Voyage and Landmark

The Voyage

The *Mayflower* was the larger of two small ships that prepared to embark from Plymouth, England, to sail to the New World on a quest for freedom. The second ship, the *Speedwell*, proved to be unfit for the long voyage across the Atlantic, so the *Mayflower* sailed alone with more than 100 men, women, and children. The voyage began in September 1620; 65 days later, on December 21, the ship anchored at Cape Cod Bay, Massachusetts.

The Landmark

Plymouth Rock is a boulder found on the shore at Plymouth, Massachusetts, where the Pilgrims first set foot in America.

Plymouth Colony Craft Activities

Let's Make a Plymouth Colony Diorama

Ask each student to bring an empty shoe box to school. Provide paint and brushes for students to paint their boxes to resemble a Plymouth community.

Reproduce the patterns on pages 24-30 for students to color, cut out, and glue inside their dioramas.

When dioramas are completed, display student projects on a table in front of your Plymouth Colony bulletin board.

Let's Make a Harvest Collage

Provide students with corrugated-board platters, scissors, markers, glue, nuts, popcorn kernels, beans, magazines, and grocery store advertisements to cut out pictures of food.

Show children how to decorate their platters and glue on pictures of favorite foods for a festive holiday decoration. Mount finished platters on colored poster board for display.

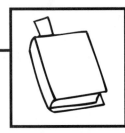

Plymouth Colony Literature Links

Who's That Stepping on Plymouth Rock?
by Jean Fritz
Coward, McCann & Geoghegan, 1975

Children will enjoy this account of the landing at Plymouth Rock.

Plymouth Rock Shape Booklets
Ask children to share thoughts of what it might have been like to travel to a new world in a ship. Then ask them to write an account of their imaginary journey from England to the New World.

Enlarge a Plymouth Rock pattern from page 30 for each child to make a cover and rock-shaped pages for a "Journey to the New World" booklet.

My Journey to the New World by Sally Grant

More Books About the First Settlers

Calico Bush
  by Rachel Field, Macmillan, 1987
Constance: A Story of Early Plymouth
  by Patricia Clapp, Lothrop, Lee & Shepard, 1968
The Double Life of Pocahontas
  by Jean Fritz, Putnam, 1983
Eating the Plates
  by Lucille Recht Penner, Macmillan, 1991
The First Thanksgiving
  by Jean Craighead George, Philomel, 1993
The First Thanksgiving Feast
  by Joan Anderson, Clarion, 1984
A New Look at the Pilgrims
  by Beatrice Siegel, Walker & Company, 1977
The Pilgrims of Plymouth
  by Marcia Sewall, Atheneum Publishers, 1986
Pocahontas
  by Ingri D'Aulaire, Doubleday, 1946
Samuel Eaton's Day
  by Kate Waters, Scholastic, 1993
Saturnalia
  by Paul Fleischman, Harper & Row, 1990

The Story of William Penn
  by Aliki, Prentice-Hall, 1964
Thanksgiving Day
  by Robert Merrill Bartlett, Crowell, 1965
The Thanksgiving Story
  by Alice Dalgliesh, Scribner's, 1988
Tituba of Salem Village
  by Ann Lane Petry, Crowell, 1964
Turkeys, Pilgrims, and Indian Corn
  by Edna Barth, Clarion, 1975
The Witch of Blackbird Pond
  by Elizabeth George Speare, Houghton Mifflin, 1961

Colonial Life in America (1650-1750)
The Thirteen Colonies

Between 1607 and 1730, the English government granted charters (limited ownership) of land to private companies and individuals to develop the New World. This resulted in the establishment and growth of the original thirteen colonies along the Atlantic coast of the United States.

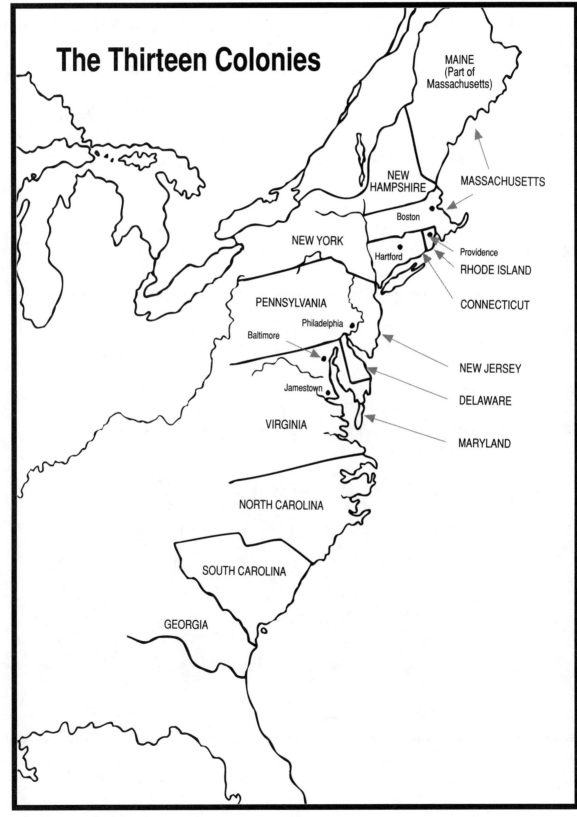

Colonial Regions
New England, the Middle Colonies, and the Southern Colonies

The New England or northern colonies grew as a result of disagreements concerning religious beliefs. Roger Williams, Thomas Hooker, and their followers moved away from the Plymouth and Massachusetts colonies to form Maine, New Hampshire, Connecticut, and Rhode Island.

The colonies continued to grow as England gained control of the middle colonies of New Amsterdam (renamed New York) and Delaware. William Penn, another Englishman seeking religious freedom, established the Pennsylvania colony. And New Jersey was founded by friends of the Duke of York.

The southern colonies developed in much the same way. Virginia was the oldest of the southern colonies, then Maryland, North and South Carolina (formerly one big colony called Carolina), and Georgia, which was the last of the original 13 to be established.

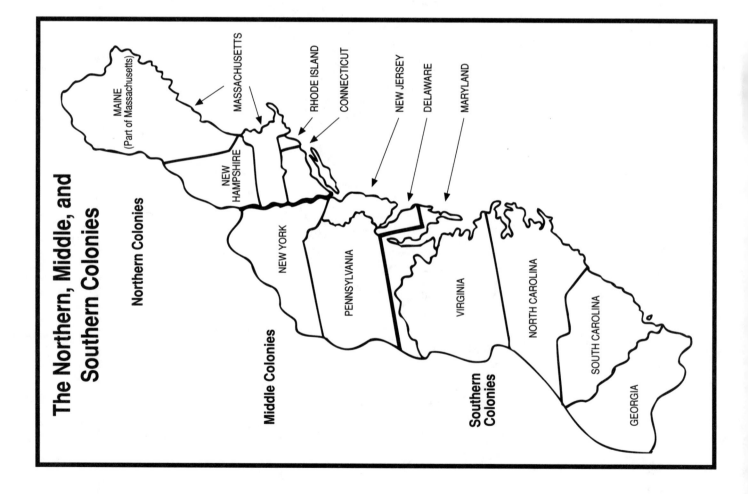

Bulletin Board: A Colonial Community

1. Enlarge the patterns on pages 36-42.
2. Color and cut out the patterns.
3. Cover your bulletin board with green paper for the ground and blue paper for the sky.
4. Add a blue bulletin board border.
5. Enlarge, color, and cut out the title below.
6. Arrange and attach the patterns to your bulletin board.

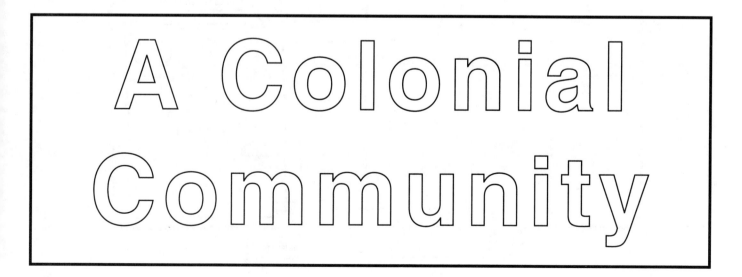

Bulletin Board Patterns:
A Dwelling in Colonial America

Dwellings in Colonial America changed from simple log structures with thatched roofs to finer brick homes with a chimney in the center. Many of the settlers built their homes to resemble those of Holland and England.

Bulletin Board Patterns:
Animals of Colonial America

Animals found in Colonial America included pigs, sheep, cows, and oxen. Oxen were used to farm land and pull supply wagons.

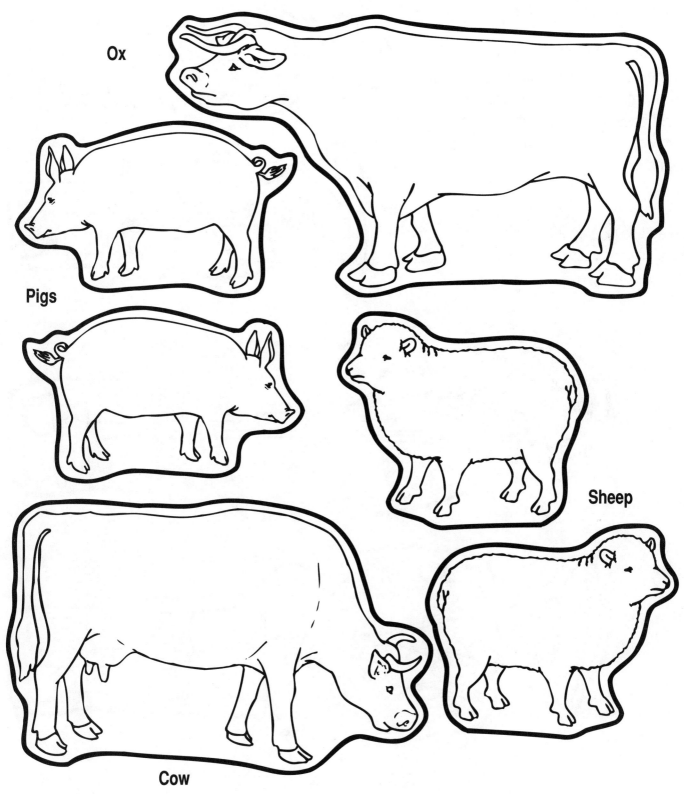

Ox

Pigs

Sheep

Cow

Bulletin Board Patterns:
People of Colonial America

Clothing of wealthy Colonial Americans and poor Colonial Americans varied greatly, as did the clothing worn by members of different religious groups.

Wealthy men wore brightly colored garments. They wore tight knee breeches, waistcoats (or vests), fancy stockings, and bright-colored leather slippers. Poorer men wore darker-colored, more simple garments.

Men also wore wigs. Wealthier men had several wigs, and often their servants wore wigs as well.

Bulletin Board Patterns:
People of Colonial America

Wealth and religious beliefs also affected the way women dressed.

Most women wore dresses with tight-fitting bodices and full skirts. Wealthy women wore colorful silk and satin dresses with hooped skirts and high-heeled shoes. They also wore several layers of lace petticoats underneath their skirts.

More Patterns for Colonial America
Food and Household Items

Colonial families produced almost everything they ate. Corn continued to be their most important food product. Other foods included rice, a variety of fruit, and fish such as haddock and cod. Tobacco and indigo, used to make dyes, were also grown in different regions.

Most utensils and tableware were made of wood or pewter. Wealthier families had household items made from glass, silver, and china.

1. **Whale-oil lamps** burned whale oil.
2. **Candle molds** were made of tin.
3. **Candle snuffers** were used to put out candles.
4. **Bed warmers** were filled with hot coals and placed under blankets.
5. **Irons** were very heavy. They were made from iron ore found in Connecticut and the middle colonies.
6. **Sugar cutters**, similar to pliers, were used to cut chunks of sugar.
7. **Butter churns** were cylinders made of hard, close-grained wood.
8. **Pipe-lighting tongs** were used to light long clay pipes.
9. **Clay pipes** were filled with tobacco or herbs for medicinal purposes.

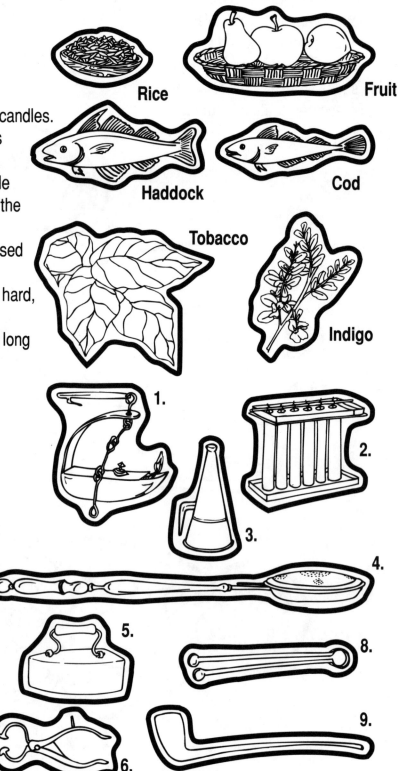

Rice

Fruit

Haddock

Cod

Tobacco

Indigo

1.

2.

3.

4.

5.

6.

7.

8.

9.

More Patterns for Colonial America
Clothing and Crafts

1. **Quilts** in a variety of designs were made by groups of women. They were used as blankets and were often family heirlooms.
2. **Spinning wheels** were used to spin thread. They were as common in Colonial homes as sewing machines are today.
3. **Wigs**, often white, were worn by men of authority as well as wealthy men. Servants often wore wigs as well.
4. **Cocked hats** were worn by most men.

1.

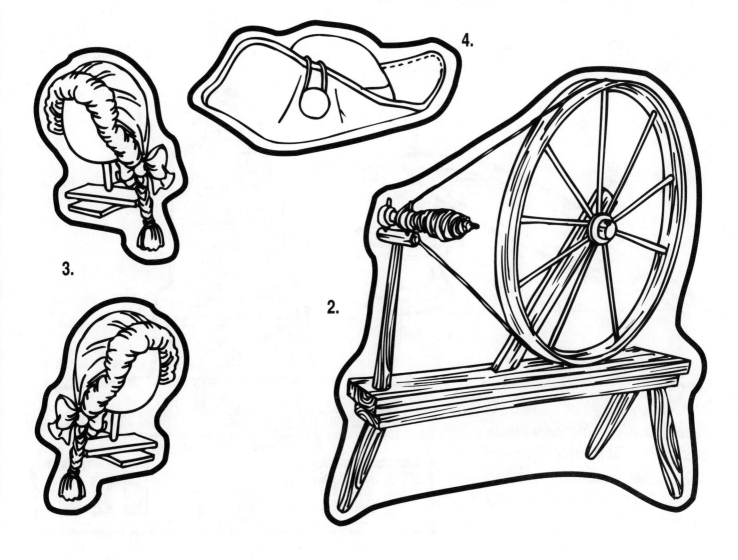

4.

3.

2.

More Patterns for Colonial America
Communication and Landmark

Quill pens made from goose feathers were used for writing. Ink wells were made to hold ink as well as for resting quill pens.

Hornbooks, made from a variety of materials, were used to protect paper used for children's lessons. Gingerbread hornbooks were made during the 1700s and children were allowed to eat letters they had learned.

In most regions letter writing and town criers were the only means of communication. In 1704, the first successful newspaper was printed in Cambridge, Massachusetts, by Stephen Daye. It was called the *Boston News-Letter.* Almanacs were also published.

In 1733, Benjamin Franklin, under the pseudonym of Richard Saunders, published the first edition of *Poor Richard's Almanac.*

Hornbook

Independence Hall

Quill pen

Ink well

Landmark
Independence Hall, also called the Old State House, was originally Britain's headquarters in the Pennsylvania colony. Later it became the location for some of the most important events in American history.

Colonial Craft Activities

Let's Make a Colonial Diorama

Ask each student to bring an empty shoe box to school. Provide paint and brushes for students to paint their boxes to resemble a Colonial community.

Reproduce the patterns on pages 36-42 for students to color, cut out, and glue inside their dioramas.

When dioramas are completed, display student projects on a table in front of your Colonial Community bulletin board.

Let's Make Colonial Hornbooks

Enlarge and reproduce the hornbook pattern for each child in your class. Provide students with poster board, scissors, markers, hole punches, and yarn to make colorful hornbooks to display their work.

For a tasty Colonial surprise, mix a batch of gingerbread dough and use the hornbook pattern as a cookie template. Once cookies are baked, use decorative frosting to write Colonial facts on the cookies.

Colonial Literature Links

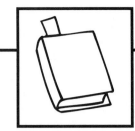

Where Was Patrick Henry on the 29th of May?
by Jean Fritz
Coward, McCann & Geoghegan, 1975

Learn about significant events in Patrick Henry's life and how he exercised his art of speaking against English laws.

Colonial Oratory Festival
Invite children to participate in a formal communication activity. Provide 18" colored poster board circles, 2" construction paper circles for hat buttons, scissors, crayons, and glue for children to make tricorn hats. Then prepare pale yellow or tan parchment speech sheets for each student to write a short speech about a favorite subject or a special event. Once all the speeches are written, have children wear their tricorn hats during the orations.

More Books About Colonial America

Amos Fortune: Free Man
    by Elizabeth Yates, Dutton, 1950
The Courage of Sarah Noble
    by Alice Dalgliesh, Scribner's, 1986
Early Thunder
    by Jean Fritz, Coward-McCann, 1967
From Colonies to Country
    by Joy Hakim, Oxford University Press, 1993
Goody Sherman's Pig
    by Mary Blount Christian, Macmillan, 1991
If You Lived in Colonial Times
    by Ann McGovern, Scholastic, 1992
Lyddie
    by Katherine Paterson, Lodestar Books, 1991
Making Thirteen Colonies
    by Joy Hakim, Oxford University Press, 1993
The Matchlock Gun
    by Walter Dumaux Edmonds, Dodd, Mead, 1941
The Story of the Thirteen Colonies
    by Clifford Lindsey Alderman, Random House, 1966

The Quest for Independence (1750-1800)
Events of the American Revolution

By winning the Revolutionary War, the 13 colonies won their freedom from British rule.

The war followed a series of conflicts that came about when the British, in need of money, created and enforced new and tougher trade laws.

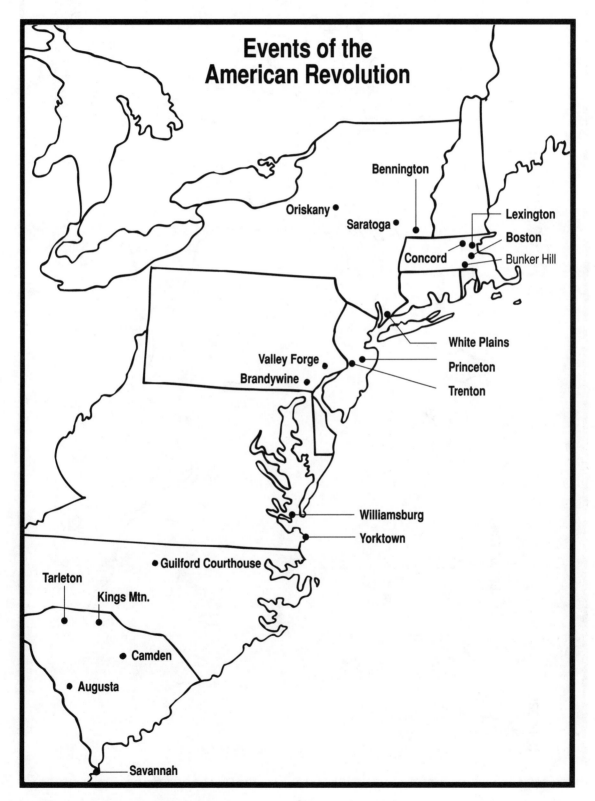

The Quest for Independence
Paul Revere's Ride

Paul Revere rode from Boston to Lexington to warn the colonists that the British were coming. A signal was to be flashed from the Old North Church: two lanterns meant the British were coming by sea, and one lantern meant they were coming by land. As expected, it was two lanterns warning that the British were crossing the Charles River in boats.

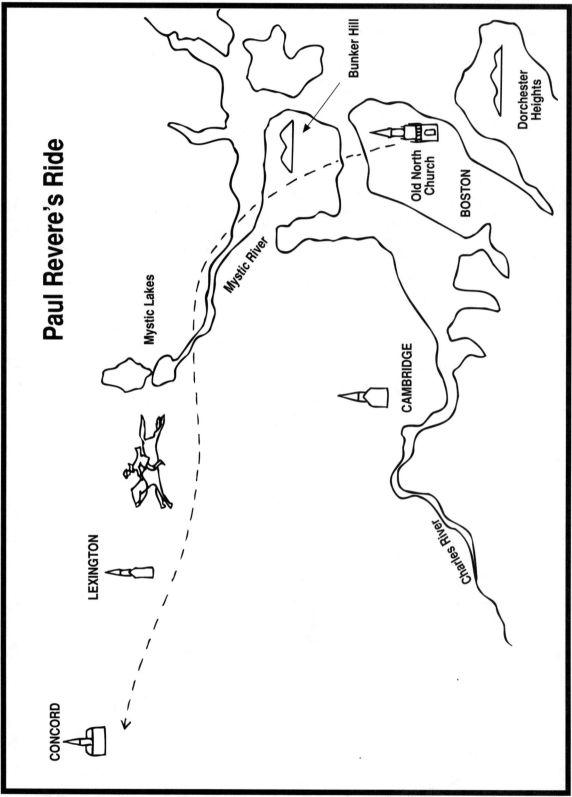

Bulletin Board:
A Community in Revolutionary Philadelphia

1. Enlarge the patterns on pages 48-54.
2. Color and cut out the patterns.
3. Cover your bulletin board with green paper for the ground and blue paper for the sky.
4. Add a red, white, and blue bulletin board border.
5. Enlarge, color, and cut out the title below.
6. Arrange and attach the patterns to your bulletin board.

Bulletin Board Patterns:
A Dwelling in Revolutionary Philadelphia

Most Revolutionary homes were brick or stone structures with two stories. The second story usually protruded over the lower story. Occasionally a fireplace was built at each end of the structure.

Bulletin Board Patterns:
Animals of Revolutionary Philadelphia

The animals found in and near Revolutionary Philadelphia included a variety of farm animals such as horses, cows, sheep, and oxen. Other animals included turkeys, opossums, rabbits, bears, minks, ermines, and raccoons. Many of these animals were hunted for food as well as for clothing. Cats were also kept to control rodents.

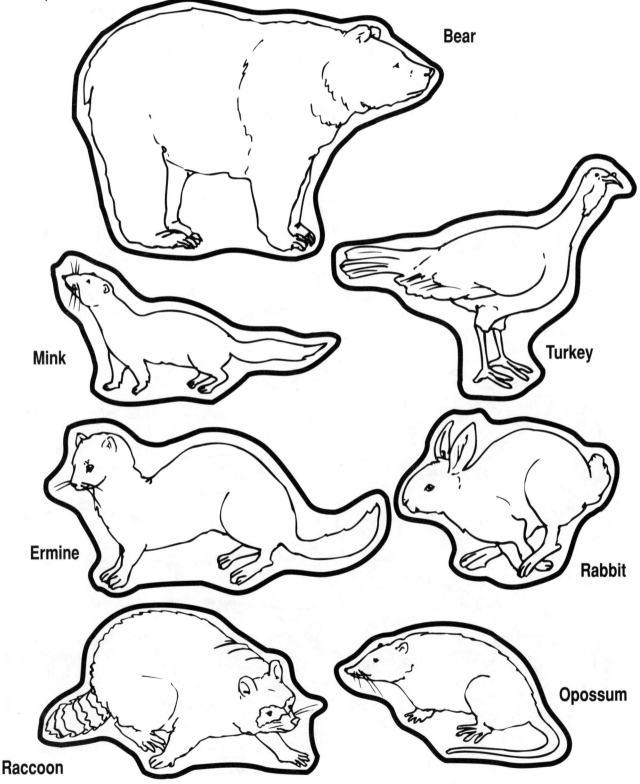

Bear

Mink

Turkey

Ermine

Rabbit

Raccoon

Opossum

Bulletin Board Patterns:
People of Revolutionary Philadelphia

Philadelphia, one of the oldest cities of the 13 colonies, was home to many wealthy and important people such as lawyers, judges, and political officials. This greatly influenced the clothing styles. Often garments were designed to imitate the elaborate styles worn by the British court and in other European countries.

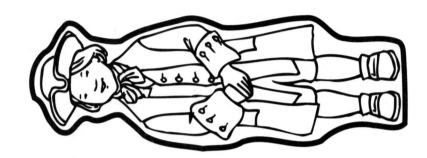

Men with official titles wore velvet coats with large cuffs, tight knee breeches, stockings, and shoes called slippers. Wigs continued to be worn by wealthy men and often their servants. Male children wore similar clothing.

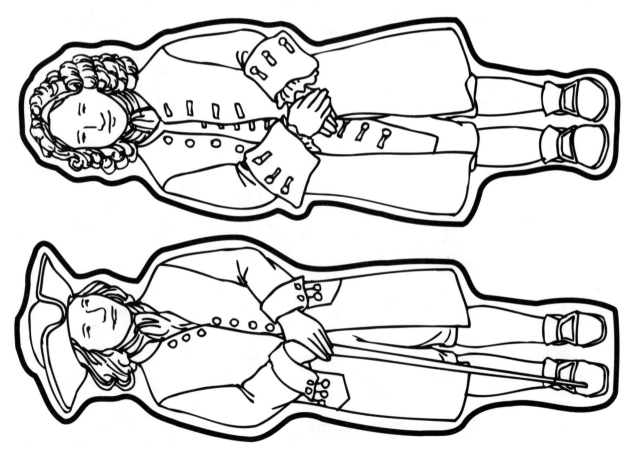

Bulletin Board Patterns:
People of Revolutionary Philadelphia

The women and girls of Philadelphia wore elaborate full-skirt dresses with several layers of lace petticoats. However, if a woman wore finer garments than her neighbors thought she should, she could be fined or arrested.

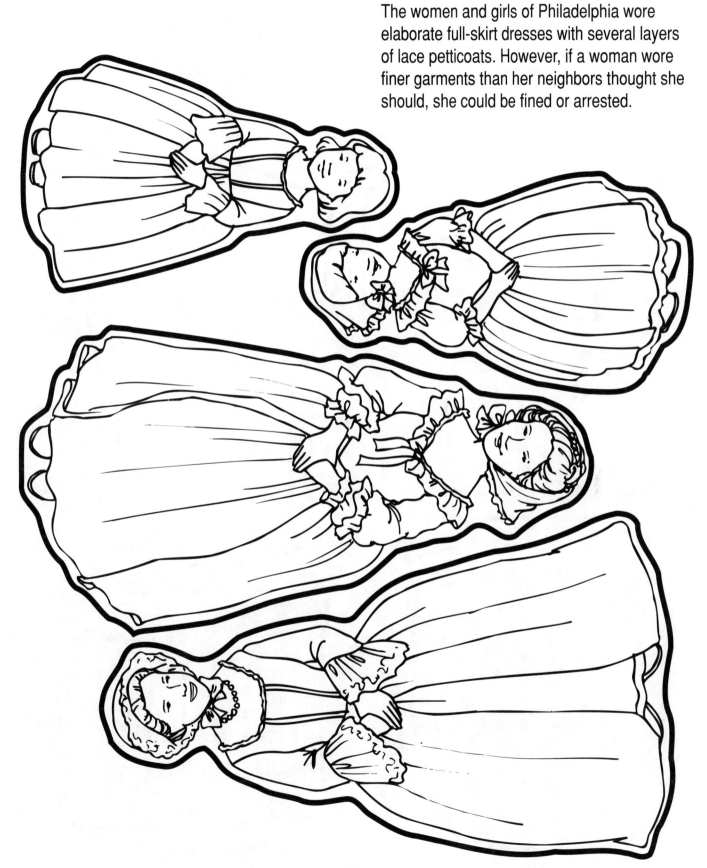

More Patterns for the American Revolution
Food, Tools, and Utensils

1. **Sugar cane** and **honey** were important products of the Colonial economy.
2. **Yokes** were used to carry wooden water buckets.
3. **Anvils** and **metalwork tools** were used by blacksmiths to make articles such as kettles, hinges, chains, and utensils.
4. **Hogsheads** were large wooden barrels used to store and transport crops such as tobacco.

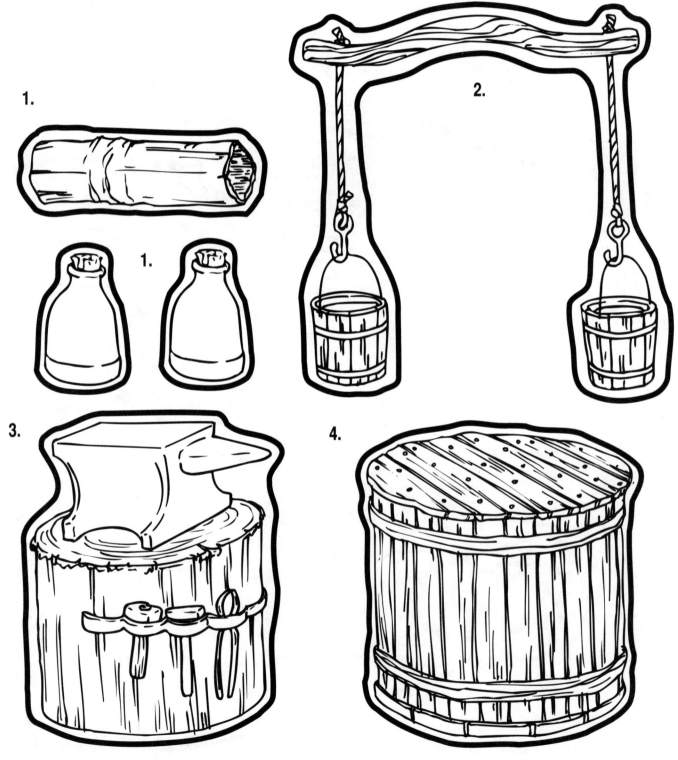

More Patterns for the American Revolution
Industry, Arts, and Crafts

1. **Sailing ships** were built from white pine and oak. The ships were used for fishing and whaling.
2. **Logging** provided businesses with wood necessary to make furniture, ships, and household items.
3. **Glassware** was first produced in the colonies in 1739.
4. **Lanterns, tankards, teapots**, and other household items were made of silver and pewter.

1.

3.

3.

3.

2.

4.

4.

4.

4.

More Patterns for the American Revolution
Weapons, Law Enforcement, and Landmarks

1. **Flintlock muskets** were used for hunting and fighting during the Revolutionary War.
2. **Leather boxes** with carrying straps were used to store and protect paper cartridges, black powder, and lead balls.
3. **Ducking stools** were used to punish gossips. The person was strapped in the seat and dunked in a pond several times.
4. **Stocks** were used to punish other offenders. The device held people by their hands, legs, and sometimes their head while they sat on hard wooden benches.

Landmarks

The **Liberty Bell** is one of the most important relics of the American Revolution. The Liberty Bell was first cast in England. It was recast in Philadelphia in 1753.

The bell was rung on July 8, 1776, calling citizens to hear the adoption of the Declaration of Independence. It was rung on the anniversary of this event every year until 1835. In July of that year it cracked while tolling for the funeral of the Chief Justice of the United States.

The **Washington Monument** was built in honor of George Washington. It stands near the Potomac River in Washington, D.C. Construction began in 1793 but the structure was not completed until 1884.

The monument is an obelisk over 500 feet tall and 55 feet along each of its four sides. The walls are 15 feet thick at the bottom and 18 inches thick at the top. The inside of the monument is hollow and the walls are set with over 100 carved historic stones.

1.

2.

Liberty Bell

Washington Monument

3.

4.

American Revolution Craft Activities

Let's Make a Revolutionary Diorama

Ask each student to bring an empty shoe box to school. Provide paint and brushes for students to paint their boxes to resemble a Revolutionary community.

Reproduce the patterns on pages 48-54 for students to color, cut out, and glue inside their dioramas.

When dioramas are completed, display student projects on a table in front of your Revolutionary Philadelphia Community bulletin board.

Let's Make an Independence Poster

Enlarge the pattern below and give one to each student to glue to a large sheet of yellow construction paper. Show how to make the edges of the paper resemble aged parchment with a brown crayon. Also provide scissors, markers, construction paper shapes, and magazines for cut-out pictures. Encourage students to design their collages to represent the freedom Americans won during the Revolution.

American Revolution Literature Links

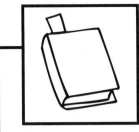

Doodle Dandy!
by Lynda Barber-Graham
Bradbury Press, 1992

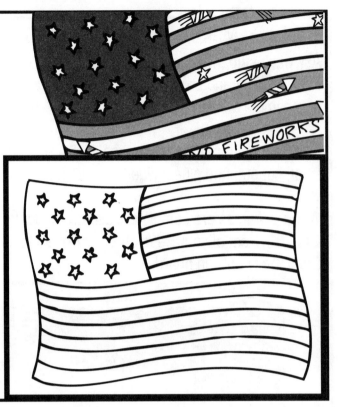

Discuss words associated with Independence Day and their significance after reading *Doodle Dandy!* with your students.

Illustrated Flags

Enlarge a flag pattern for each child and provide scissors and markers. Instruct children to choose a word to illustrate on the stripes of the flag. Display finished flags along the top of your bulletin and chalk boards.

More Books About the American Revolution

And Then What Happened, Paul Revere?
by Jean Fritz, Coward, 1973

Black Heroes of the American Revolution
by Burke Davis, Harcourt Brace Jovanovich, 1976

The Boston Coffee Party
by Doreen Rappaport, Harper & Row, 1988

Can't You Make Them Behave, King George?
by Jean Fritz, Coward, 1977

The Great Little Madison
by Jean Fritz, Coward, 1989

John Treegate's Musket
by Leonard Wibberley, Farrar, Straus & Giroux, 1969

Johnny Tremain
by Esther Forbes, Houghton Mifflin, 1943

Meet Felicity
by Valerie Tripp, Pleasant Company, 1991

Mr. Revere and I
by Robert Lawson, Little, Brown, 1953

My Brother Sam Is Dead
by James Lincoln Collier & Christopher Collier, Four Winds Press, 1974

The New Nation
by Joy Hakim, Oxford University Press, 1993

Paul Revere
by Martin Lee, Watts, 1987

Sara Bishop
by Scott O'Dell, Houghton Mifflin, 1980

This Time Tempe Wick
by Patricia Lee Gauch, Coward, 1974

USKids History: Book of the American Revolution
by Howard Egger-Bovet and Marlene Smith-Baranzini, Little, Brown, 1994

War Comes to Willy Freeman
by James Lincoln Collier & Christopher Collier, Delacorte, 1983

What's the Big Idea, Ben Franklin?
by Jean Fritz, Coward, 1976

Why Don't You Get a Horse, Sam Adams?
by Jean Fritz, Coward, 1974

Will You Sign Here, John Hancock?
by Jean Fritz, Coward, 1976

Westward Bound (1800-1850)

America Moves West

Daring pioneers of early America made it possible for travel to the western regions of the United States. The move west took place in several stages, from 1783 through 1854.

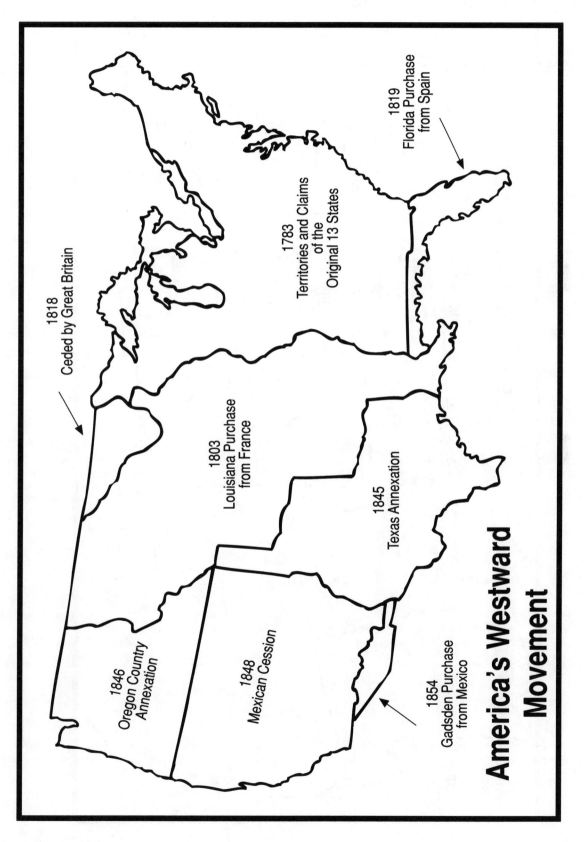

1819
Florida Purchase
from Spain

1783
Territories and Claims
of the
Original 13 States

1818
Ceded by Great Britain

1803
Louisiana Purchase
from France

1845
Texas Annexation

1846
Oregon Country
Annexation

1848
Mexican Cession

1854
Gadsden Purchase
from Mexico

America's Westward Movement

Westward Bound
Lewis and Clark Expedition

Captains Meriwether Lewis and William Clark were chosen by President Thomas Jefferson to blaze a new trail to the Pacific Ocean. They began their 8,000-mile journey in May 1804, in St. Louis, Missouri, and reached the Pacific in November of 1805.

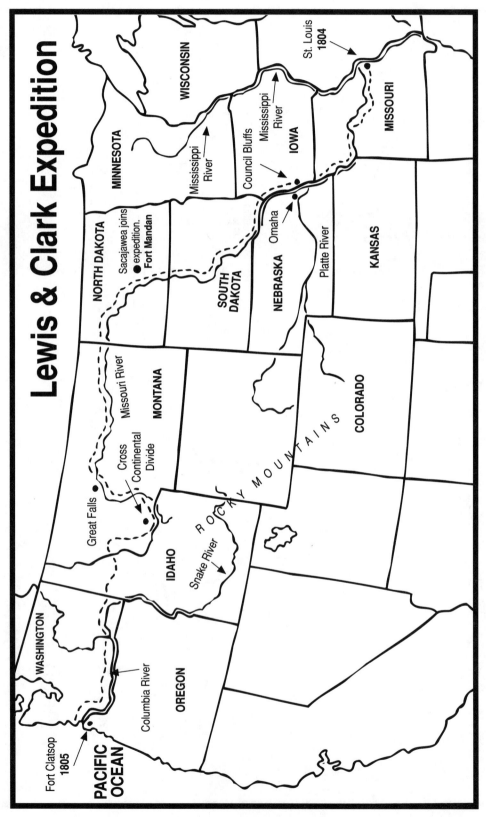

Bulletin Board: A Western Frontier Community

1. Enlarge the patterns on pages 60-66.
2. Color and cut out the patterns.
3. Cover your bulletin board with tan paper for the ground and blue paper for the sky.
4. Add a brown bulletin board border.
5. Enlarge, color, and cut out the title below.
6. Arrange and attach the patterns to your bulletin board.

A Western Frontier Community

Bulletin Board Patterns:
A Western Frontier Dwelling

The pioneers of the western frontier, like the first settlers of the New World, used the resources available to them to survive. Many frontier homes, called log cabins, were structures built from rough cut trees.

Bulletin Board Patterns:
Animals of the Western Frontier

Animals, birds, and fish found on the frontier included foxes, jack rabbits, salmon, prairie dogs, polecats, magpies, horses, and buffalo.

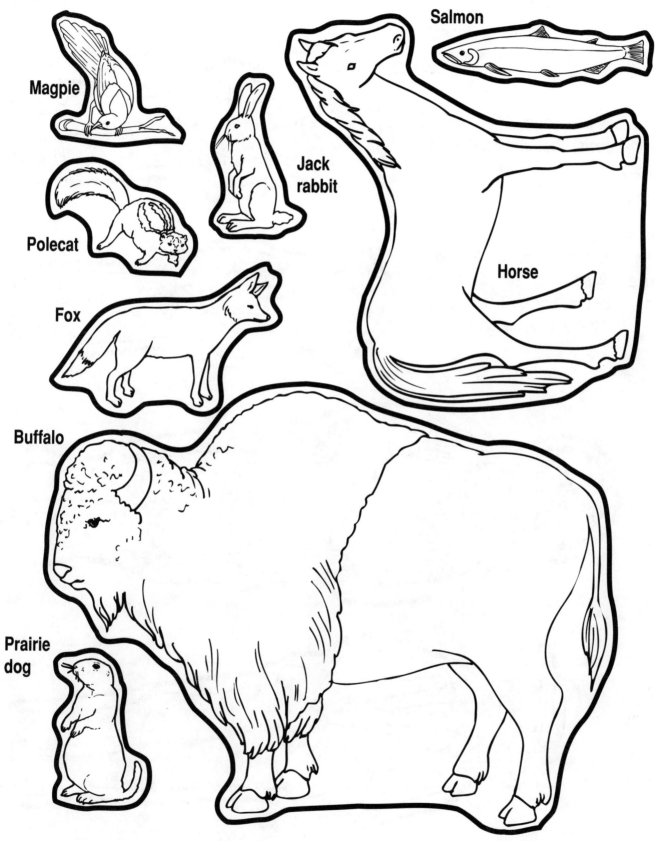

Salmon

Magpie

Polecat

Jack rabbit

Horse

Fox

Buffalo

Prairie dog

Bulletin Board Patterns:
People of the Western Frontier

The pioneers' clothing was somewhat different from that worn by people who lived in eastern cities. Garments made from woven cloth or animal skins were simple and functional.

Men and boys wore shirts, denim pants, and leather boots. They also wore coats and hats. Some men wore garments made from animal skins.

Leather pullover shirts were worn as coats. Most were designed with fringed sleeves and hems. Pants sometimes had fringed side seams. Some pioneers wore fur coats and caps during the cold winter months.

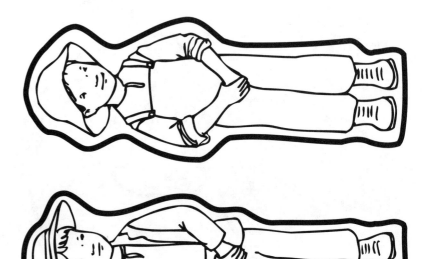

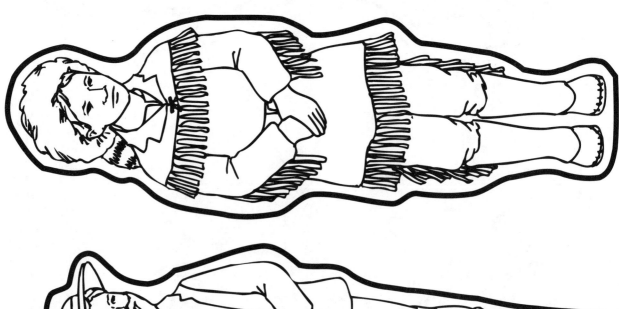

Bulletin Board Patterns:
People of the Western Frontier

Women and girls wore simple yet functional dresses. They also wore aprons and bonnets to protect themselves from the weather.

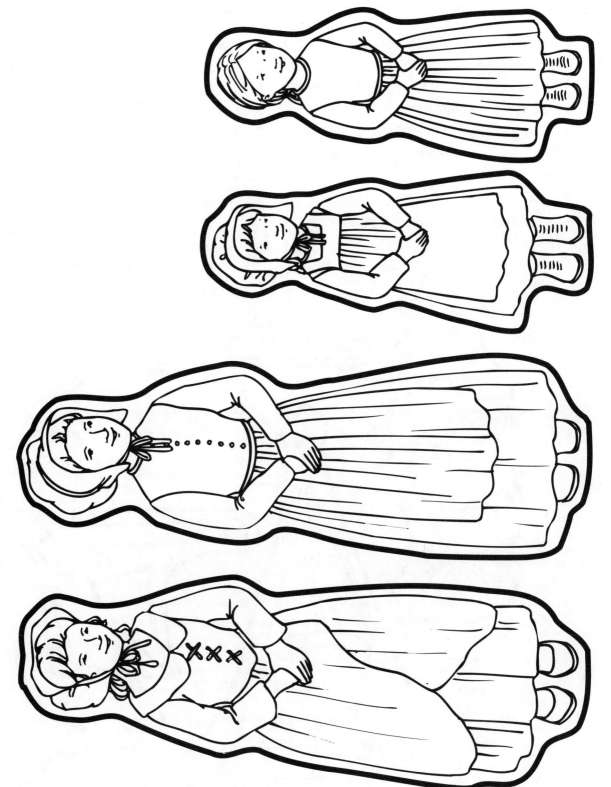

More Patterns for the Western Frontier
Food, Plants, and Supplies

Pioneers hunted for much of their food. This made carrying a rifle very important. Food was cooked in iron pots over open fires.

Some families continued the perilous journey further west while others established new farming settlements in what is now the Midwest. Farmers grew corn, wheat, and cotton.

1. **Cactus plants** were first seen by pioneers as they traveled west.
2. **Rifles** were important to every pioneer family for protection as well as hunting.
3. **Steel plows**, invented by John Deere in 1834, were used to till soil for crops in farming settlements.
4. **Animal pelts**, or furs, were traded for supplies and used to make garments.

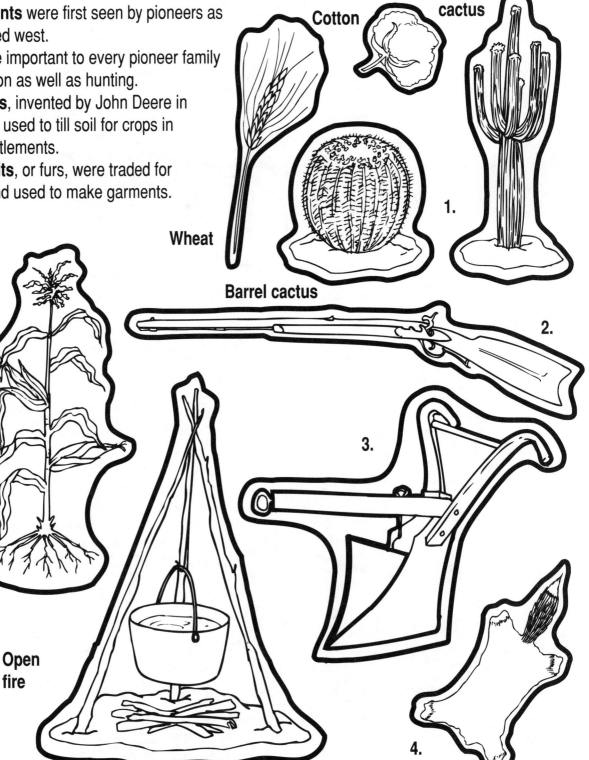

Cotton

Saguaro cactus

Wheat

Barrel cactus

Corn

Open fire

1.

2.

3.

4.

More Patterns for the Western Frontier
Industry and Inventions

1. **Colt revolvers**, invented in 1835 by Samuel Colt, were the first successful repeating pistols.
2. **Cotton gins**, invented by Eli Whitney, were used to separate cotton fiber from the seed. The use of this machine made cotton the chief crop of the southern states.
3. **Harpoon guns** were used to hunt whales. Whaling was an important industry, since whales provided oil for lamps and whalebones for dressmaking.
4. **Reapers** were used to harvest grain. Cyrus McCormick invented the first reaper in 1834.
5. **Telegraphs** were used to send messages more quickly over long distances. Many people were responsible for the invention of the telegraph. On May 24, 1844, Samuel F. B. Morse sent the following historical telegraph message: "What hath God wrought!"

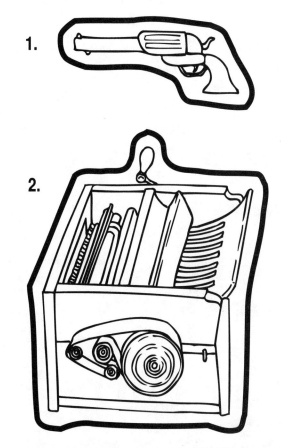

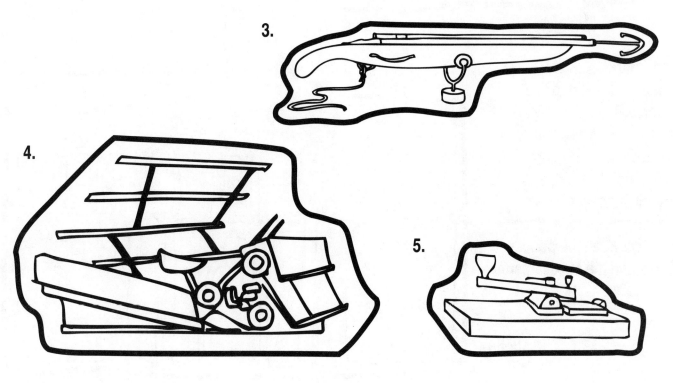

More Patterns for the Western Frontier

Transportation and Landmark

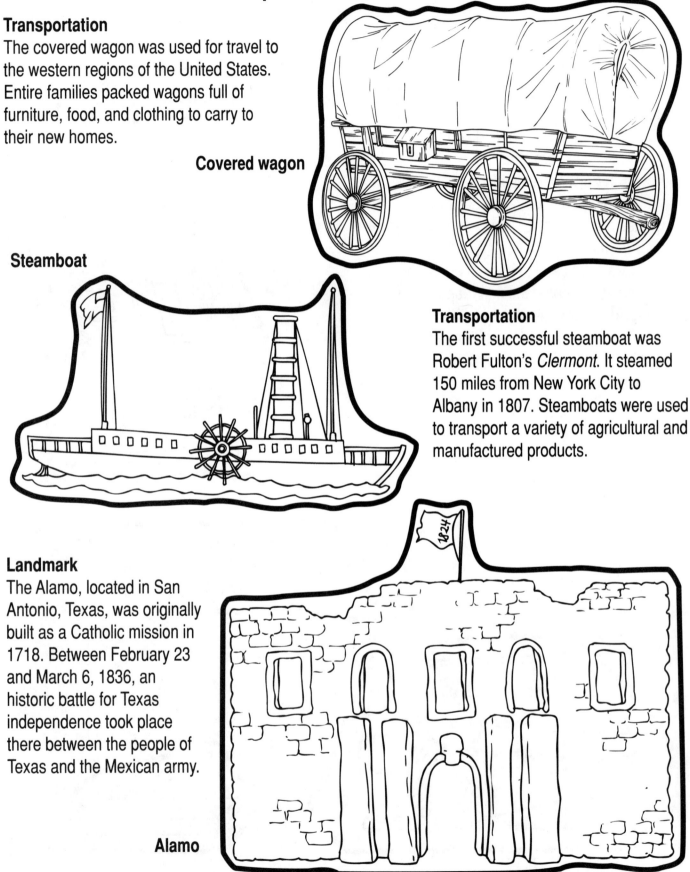

Transportation

The covered wagon was used for travel to the western regions of the United States. Entire families packed wagons full of furniture, food, and clothing to carry to their new homes.

Covered wagon

Steamboat

Transportation

The first successful steamboat was Robert Fulton's *Clermont*. It steamed 150 miles from New York City to Albany in 1807. Steamboats were used to transport a variety of agricultural and manufactured products.

Landmark

The Alamo, located in San Antonio, Texas, was originally built as a Catholic mission in 1718. Between February 23 and March 6, 1836, an historic battle for Texas independence took place there between the people of Texas and the Mexican army.

Alamo

Western Frontier Craft Activities

Let's Make a Western Frontier Diorama

Ask each student to bring an empty shoe box to school. Provide paint and brushes for students to paint their boxes to resemble a western frontier community.

Reproduce the patterns on pages 60-66 for students to color, cut out, and glue inside their dioramas.

When dioramas are completed, display student projects on a table in front of your Western Frontier Community bulletin board.

Let's Make an Oatmeal Box Wagon Train

Ask children to bring empty oatmeal and tissue boxes, brown grocery bags, and cloth scraps to school for a wagon train classroom project. Provide students with construction paper, corrugated and poster board, scissors, crayons, and glue. Show how to assemble the tissue and oatmeal boxes. Then show how to cut out and attach corrugated board wheels and the wagon cloth cover. Have each child make up and write a name or slogan on his or her wagon. Place the wagons around the perimeter of a Western Frontier book corner.

OATMEAL

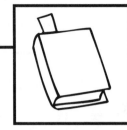

Western Frontier Literature Links

Eight Hands Round
by Ann Whitford Paul
HarperCollins, 1991

Learn about Early American patchwork quilt designs and their origins.

Patchwork Autobiographies
Provide each student with twelve 8" colored construction paper squares and magazines for cut-out pictures to make a patchwork autobiography. Encourage children to add photographs, cloth scraps, and other articles such as baseball cards, stickers, or greeting cards to their quilt patches. When quilt patches are finished, have students punch four holes along the sides of each patch. Then show how to lace and finish the outside edges with yarn.

More Books About the Western Frontier

A Family Apart
by Joan Lowery Nixon, Bantam Books, 1987
Johnny Appleseed
by Steven Kellogg, Morrow Junior Books, 1988
Johnny Appleseed
by Reeve Lindbergh, Little, Brown, 1990
Jump Ship to Freedom
by James Lincoln Collier & Christopher Collier, Delacorte, 1981
Laura Ingalls Wilder
by William T. Anderson, HarperCollins, 1992
Let's Be Early Settlers with Daniel Boone
by Peggy Parrish, Harper & Row, 1967
The Little House Cookbook
by Barbara Muhs Walker, Harper & Row, 1979
Little House in the Big Woods
by Laura Ingalls Wilder, Harper & Row, 1953
Make Way for Sam Houston
by Jean Fritz, Putnam's, 1986
Meet Kirsten
by Janet Shaw, Pleasant Company, 1986
Old Yeller
by Frederick Benjamin Gipson, Harper & Row, 1956

Prairie Songs
by Pam Conrad, Harper & Row, 1985
Prairie Visions: The Life and Times of Solomon Butcher
by Pam Conrad, HarperCollins, 1991
Quit Pulling My Leg! A Story of Davy Crockett
by Robert M. Quackenbush, Prentice-Hall, 1987
Sarah, Plain and Tall
by Patricia MacLachlan, Harper & Row, 1985
The Story of the Louisiana Purchase
by Mary Kay Phelan, Crowell, 1979
Wagon Wheels
by Barbara Brenner, Harper & Row, 1978
Who Is Carrie?
by James Lincoln Collier & Christopher Collier, Delacorte, 1984
The Young United States
by Edwin Tunis, Crowell, 1976

Laura Ingalls Wilder

The Gold Rush Years (1850-1875)
Gold Mining Territories

The word "gold" increased westward movement. People traveled by foot, horseback, and boat in search of fortunes. Towns seemed to grow up overnight as more people filled the regions around gold rush territories. Gold seekers traveled as far as the Klondike River in Canada's Yukon.

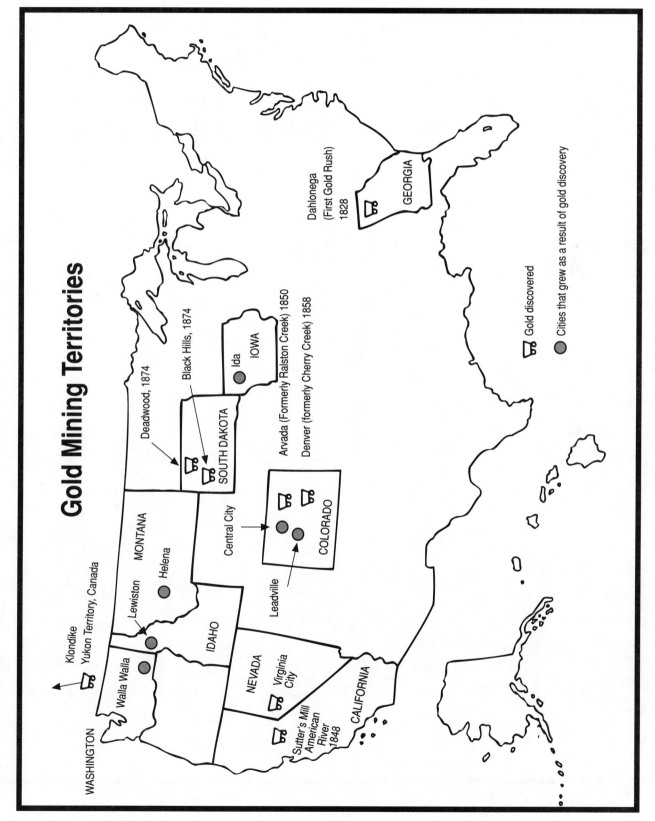

California Gold Rush

Nearly 100,000 people rushed to California during the 1849 gold rush.

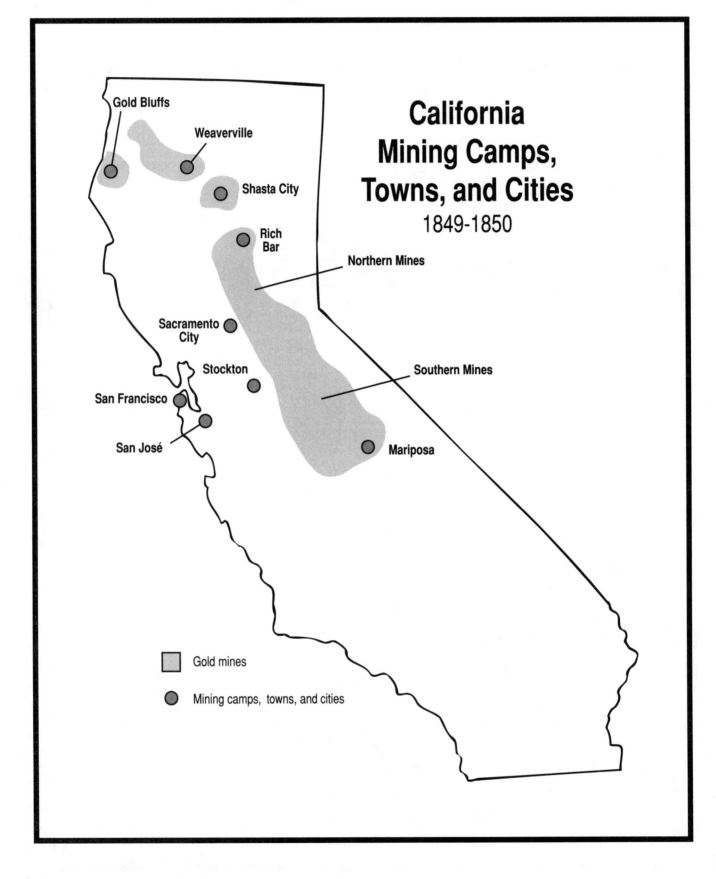

California Mining Camps, Towns, and Cities
1849-1850

Gold Bluffs

Weaverville

Shasta City

Rich Bar

Northern Mines

Sacramento City

Southern Mines

Stockton

San Francisco

San José

Mariposa

☐ Gold mines

● Mining camps, towns, and cities

Bulletin Board: A Gold Rush Community

1. Enlarge the patterns on pages 72-78.
2. Color and cut out the patterns.
3. Cover your bulletin board with tan paper for the ground and blue paper for the sky.
4. Cut gray and brown rocks in a variety of sizes and attach to the board.
5. Add a gold bulletin board border.
6. Enlarge, color, and cut out the title below.
7. Arrange and attach the patterns to your bulletin board.

Bulletin Board Patterns: A Gold Rush Dwelling

Many people who traveled west in search of gold traveled in wagon trains. Entire families lived out of wagons covered with heavy cloth. Furniture, household supplies, and food were transported in the wagons along with weapons for hunting and gold mining tools.

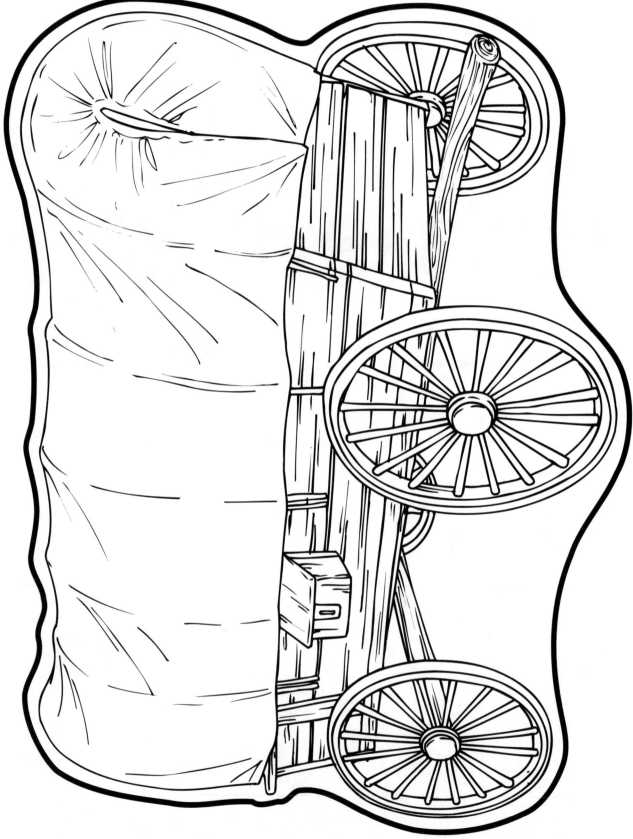

Bulletin Board Patterns:
Animals of a Gold Rush Community

Gold seekers encountered a variety of animals and birds as they traveled west, including pheasant, ruffed grouse, prairie chickens, sheep, and elk. Other animals seen during the gold rush years were donkeys and mules. They were used to carry heavy loads, including gold.

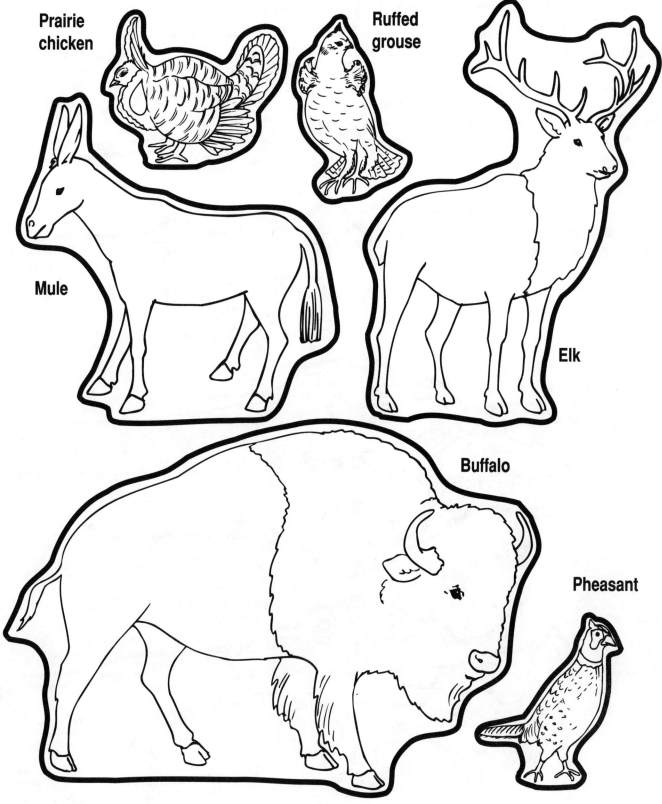

Prairie chicken

Ruffed grouse

Mule

Elk

Buffalo

Pheasant

Bulletin Board Patterns:
People of a Gold Rush Community

Clothing worn by frontier families had to be sturdy and serviceable. Sometimes many months would pass before settlers were able to buy supplies to repair or replace torn and worn-out garments. Shoes were important clothing items. Most everyone wore shoes during the winter months, though children often went barefoot during the summer.

Men and boys wore shirts, denim pants, vests, and heavy leather boots. They also wore hats to protect them from the hot and cold weather. Sometimes men wore bandanas, or scarves tied around their necks. These scarves were used to cover their faces against wind and sandstorms as they traveled through different regions.

Bulletin Board Patterns:
People of a Gold Rush Community

Women were responsible for all the domestic chores. Sometimes farming and hunting were part of their daily tasks as well.

Women and girls wore checkered or patchwork dresses. Women's dresses had long skirts while girls' dresses were often calf-length. Women and girls also wore aprons and bonnets to protect themselves from the weather.

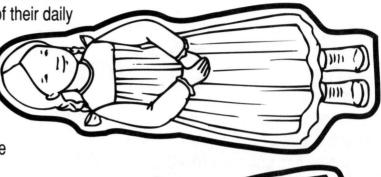

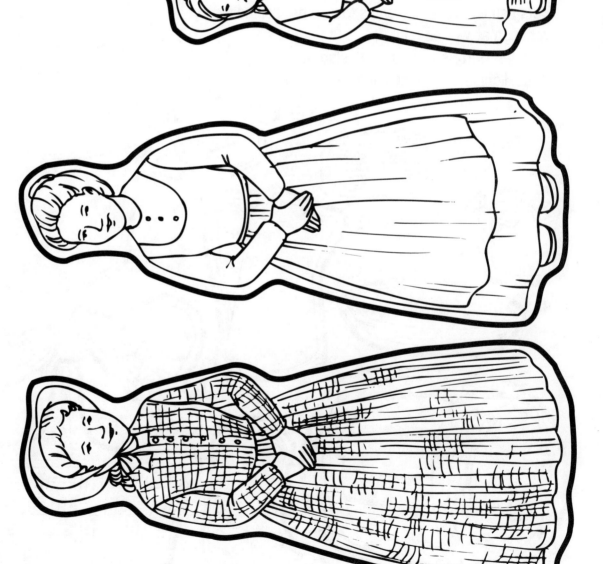

More Patterns for the Gold Rush
Food, Clothing, and Utensils

Meals generally included one or all of the following foods: bread, bacon, dried beans, salt pork, and flapjacks.

1. **Coffee pots** were important to every family and prospector. Coffee was often the only liquid they drank.
2. **Iron skillets** were used to cook flapjacks and other foods.
3. **Iron pots** were used to cook beans, stews, and other foods.
4. **Tin plates** and **cups** were used to serve food. They were unbreakable.
5. **Baskets** held dried foods and were storage containers for needed supplies.
6. **Boots** were made from leather.
7. **Hats** usually had broad brims to help protect the wearer from sun as well as rain.
8. **Wooden barrels** were used to store and transport foods, liquids, and sometimes gunpowder.

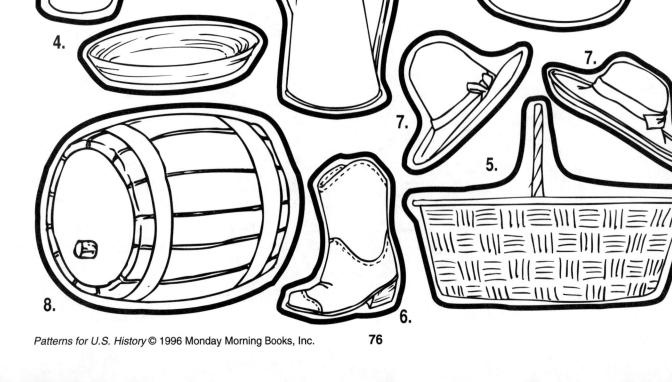

Bread

Flapjacks

Beans

Salt pork

Bacon

2.

2.

4.

1.

3.

4.

7.

7.

5.

8.

6.

More Patterns for the Gold Rush
Tools

Every gold rush family or individual needed a variety of tools to look for and mine gold.

1. **Axe**
2. **Shovels**
3. **Wooden trays** were used to hold diggings and sort through dirt.
4. **Pick axes** were used in hard-to-reach places during digging or mining.
5. **Dynamite** was used to blast rocks. It was also used to excavate gold mines.
6. **Spurs** were worn just above boot heels to urge horses to move.
7. **Barbed wire** was invented by Joseph F. Glidden in 1873. It was used to secure land boundaries. The use of barbed wire was also the cause of many range wars.
8. **Gold miners** often sat along creek beds and other bodies of water. They used **pans** to sift dirt and rocks from streams to find gold particles. This was called "panning for gold."

More Patterns for the Gold Rush
Communication, Transportation, and Landmark

Communication

Real estate posters were displayed in many new settlements and newly established towns. Often the posters would advertise land for homesteaders.

Transportation

Stagecoaches were one form of transportation in the west. Stagecoaches carried payrolls, merchandise, and people between major cities. Railroads, which linked the east to the west, were the most important form of transportation during this period. Thousands of Chinese, Irish, Scottish, German, and Scandinavian immigrants worked to extend the railways to the Pacific.

Landmark

On May 10, 1869, the tracks of the Union Pacific and the Central Pacific were joined at Promontory, Utah. A golden spike was driven where the two rail lines met as a symbol of the completion of the first railroad to span the United States. The golden spike is now on display at Stanford University in Palo Alto, California.

Stagecoach

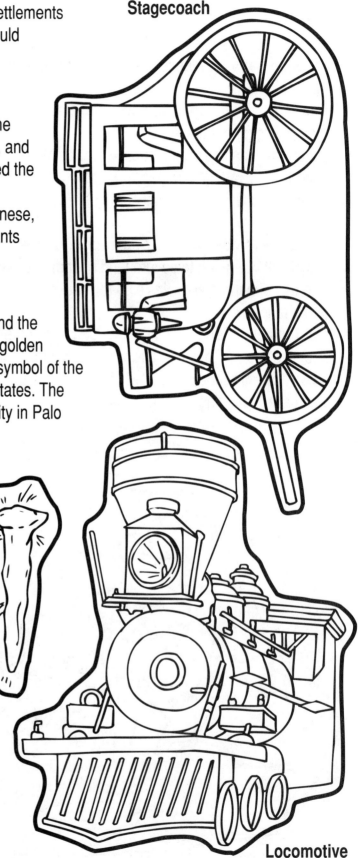

Golden spike

Real estate poster

FARMS AND HOMES IN KANSAS
EMIGRANTS
LOOK TO YOUR
INTERESTS
FARMS AT $3. PER ACRE!
AND NOT A FOOT OF WASTELAND.
FARMS ON TEN YEARS' CREDIT
Lands not Taxable for Six Years!
FARMING LANDS IN
EASTERN KANSAS

Locomotive

Gold Rush Craft Activities

Let's Make a Gold Rush Diorama

Ask each student to bring an empty shoe box to school. Provide paint and brushes for students to paint their boxes to resemble a gold rush community.

Reproduce the patterns on pages 72-78 for students to color, cut out, and glue inside their dioramas.

When dioramas are completed, display student projects on a table in front of your Gold Rush Community bulletin board.

Let's Make Papier Mache Gold Nuggets

Provide students with small paper bags, newspaper, paint, brushes, and a glue solution.

Show children how to stuff their bags and then wrap them with glue-dipped newspaper strips to form a nugget. Allow the nuggets to dry, then have children paint their nuggets with yellow, orange, and patches of green.

Invite children to invent gold strike stories using their nuggets as visual aids.

Gold Rush Literature Links

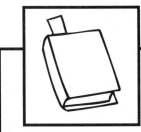

Chang's Paper Pony
by E. Coerr
Harper & Row, 1988

Share this story about how a Chinese boy named Chang, who works with his grandfather in a mining camp kitchen, gets the pony of his dreams.

Dream Pony Bonanza
Enlarge a pony pattern for each child and provide scissors and markers or crayons to make his or her dream pony. Display finished ponies on a bulletin board entitled "My Dream Pony."

More Books About the Gold Rush

By the Great Horn Spoon!
by Sid Fleishman, Little, Brown, 1963
The Chinese Americans
by Milton Meltzer, Crowell, 1980
Fool's Gold
by Zilpha Keatley Snyder, Delacorte Press, 1993
Gold! The Klondike Adventure
by Delta Ray, Lodestar, 1989
The Great American Gold Rush
by Rhoda Blunberg, Bradbury Press, 1989
Snowshoe Thompson
by Nancy Smiler Levinson, HarperCollins, 1992

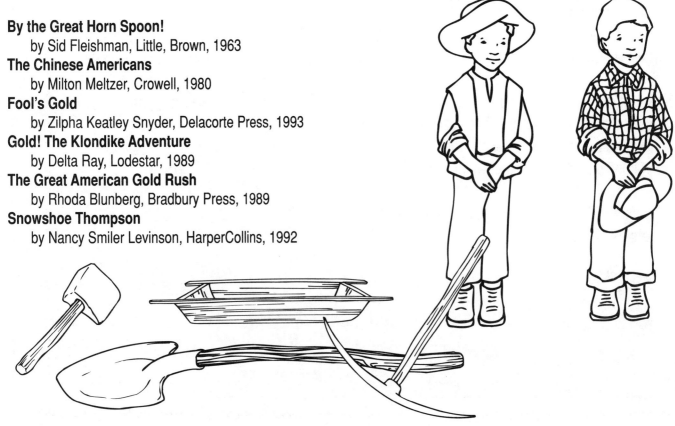

A Nation Divided—The Civil War (1861-1865)
Pre-Civil War United States

The Civil War was the first modern war. It took more American lives than any other war in history. Many people thought the war would last only a few months. But it went on to last more than four years.

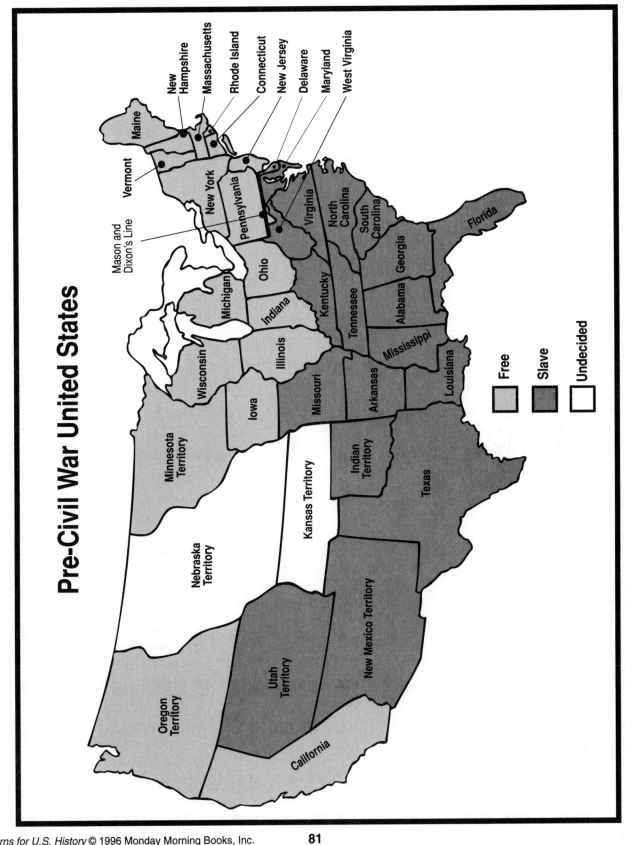

Battlefields of the North and the South

The Civil War began on April 12, 1861, when the Confederate army attacked Fort Sumter in Charleston, South Carolina. Eleven states fought under the Confederate flag and 23 states fought under the Union flag.

Battlefields of the Civil War

ALABAMA
Montgomery
Mobile

FLORIDA
Jacksonville
St. Augustine

GEORGIA
Chickamauga
Atlanta

ILLINOIS
Cairo

KENTUCKY
Perryville

LOUISIANA
Valverde
New Orleans

MARYLAND
Antietam (Sharpsburg)
Monocacy
Baltimore
Washington

MISSISSIPPI
Luka
Vicksburg

MISSOURI
Pilot Knob
Wilson's Creek

PENNSYLVANIA
Gettysburg
Philadelphia

SOUTH CAROLINA
Ft. Sumter

TENNESSEE
Nashville
Murfreesboro
Chattanooga
Memphis
Shiloh

VIRGINIA
Appomattox Court House
New Market
Manassas
Groveton
Brandy Station
Fredericksburg
Richmond
Seven Pines
Petersburg
The Wilderness
Hampton Roads
    (Monitor and Merrimac)

WEST VIRGINIA
Harpers Ferry
Winchester

Bulletin Board: A Civil War Community

1. Enlarge the patterns on pages 84-90.
2. Color and cut out the patterns.
3. Cover your bulletin board with gray and blue paper.
4. Enlarge the flag patterns on page 90 and attach one to either side of the board.
5. Add a blue and gray bulletin board border.
6. Enlarge, color, and cut out the title below.
7. Arrange and attach the patterns to your bulletin board.

Bulletin Board Patterns: A Civil War Dwelling

Dwellings of Civil War America varied from region to region. Those found on southern plantations were often elaborate two-story brick structures. Most houses had front porches lined with huge columns.

Bulletin Board Patterns:
Animals of a Civil War Community

The animals found in Civil War communities of the South included horses, sheep, and donkeys.

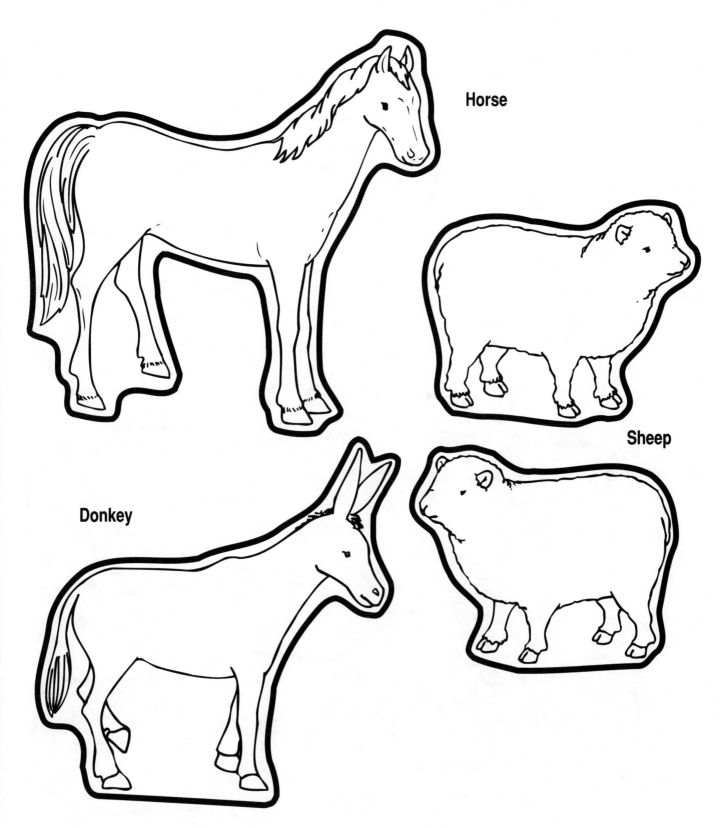

Horse

Sheep

Donkey

Bulletin Board Patterns:
People of a Civil War Community

Clothing differed between regions, the wealthy and the poor, and the slaves and the free. Wealthy people, including plantation and slave owners, wore fine garments, while slaves dressed in simple, often old or worn clothing.

Free men wore long pants, shirts, vests, hats, and coats. Slave men and boys wore pants and shirts. Many slaves went without shoes.

Military officers wore fine uniforms consisting of pants, shirts, long coats, and broad-brimmed hats. Union soldiers wore blue uniforms and Confederate soldiers wore gray.

Bulletin Board Patterns:
People of a Civil War Community

Wealthy women wore elaborate dresses with hoop skirts. Dresses were decorated with satin ribbons, lace, and embroidery. The women also wore bonnets, a variety of hair ornaments, and shawls draped over their shoulders. Slave women and girls wore very plain and simple dresses. Many wore tattered dresses. Most did not have shoes.

More Patterns for the Civil War Years
Industry

Sugar cane, wheat, flour, tobacco, cotton, and coal were important products of Civil War America. As the war continued, many of these and other products became luxury items. Flour sometimes sold for $300 a barrel, and even shoes cost as much as $200 a pair.

Steel was also an important product of the time. Steel production increased as the need for war weapons and equipment grew.

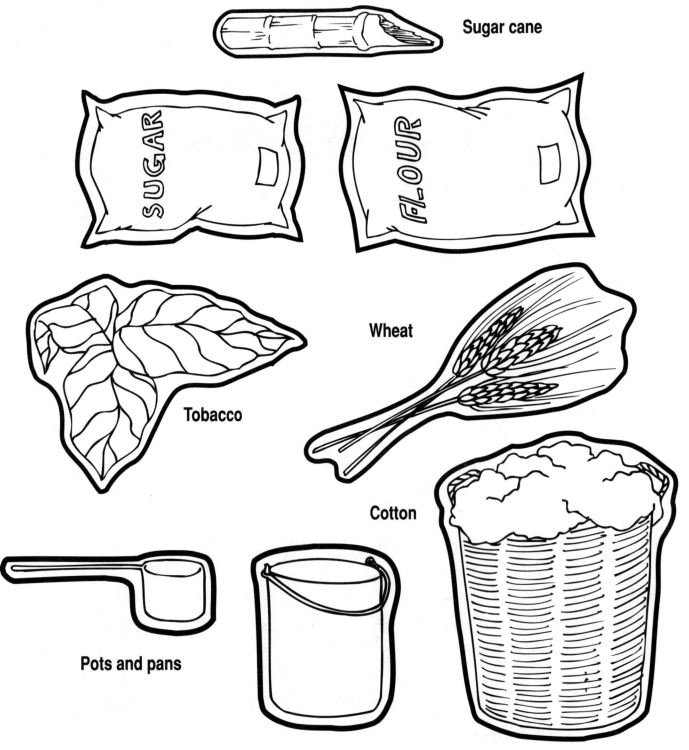

Sugar cane

SUGAR

FLOUR

Tobacco

Wheat

Cotton

Pots and pans

More Patterns for the Civil War Years
War Materials and Equipment

1. **Caps** were worn by both Union and Confederate soldiers.
2. **Rifles** and **sabres** were soldiers' weapons.
3. **Cannons** were used for long-distance attacks.
4. **The bugle** and the **drum** were important during the war. They were used to communicate general orders as well as to boost morale as soldiers entered into battles.

Confederate hat

1.

Union hat

1.

2.

2.

3.

4.

4.

More Patterns for the Civil War Years
Communication and Landmark

The United States was a divided nation during the Civil War years. Even the nation's symbols were divided, instead of one there were two flags.

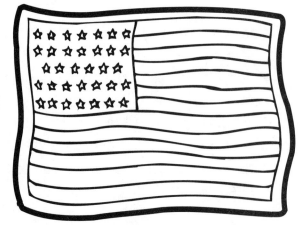

The Union continued to fly a traditional flag. In 1861 the flag had 34 stars representing both the northern and southern states. The Confederacy's flag was a different shape and design. It was square and had 11 stars for 11 southern states, plus 2 for Kentucky and Missouri's secessionist governments.

The Emancipation Proclamation is an important historic document. It was written in 1863 by Abraham Lincoln. It reinforced the principals of the Declaration of Independence—that "all men are created equal"—and declared slaves free.

Emancipation Proclamation

hereas, on the twenty-second day of September, in the year of our Lord one thousand eight hundred and sixty-two, a proclamation was issued by the President of the United States, containing, among other things, the following, to wit:

Landmark
The Lincoln Memorial in Washington, D.C., was completed in 1922 in honor of the sixteenth president of the United States, Abraham Lincoln. In the center of this structure is a great hall with three decorated sections. A gigantic statue of Lincoln sits in the center section.

Civil War Craft Activities

Let's Make a Civil War Diorama

Ask each student to bring an empty shoe box to school. Provide paint and brushes for students to paint their boxes to resemble a Civil War community.

Reproduce the patterns on pages 84-90 for students to color, cut out, and glue inside their dioramas.

When dioramas are completed, display student projects on a table in front of your Civil War Community bulletin board.

Let's Make a Freedom Train

Create a Freedom Train to display around the walls of your classroom to reinforce a unit on heroes and heroines who were involved with the Underground Railroad.

Enlarge, color, and cut out the engine pattern and then reproduce an enlarged box car pattern for each child to color and cut out.

Instruct children to write facts about events or people related to the Underground Railroad on their cars.

Welcome Aboard the Freedom Train

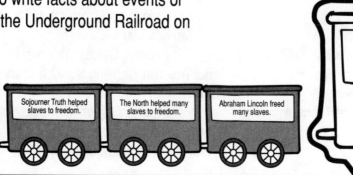

Welcome Aboard the Freedom Train

Sojourner Truth helped slaves to freedom.

The North helped many slaves to freedom.

Abraham Lincoln freed many slaves.

Civil War Literature Links

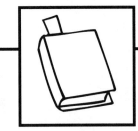

True Stories About Abraham Lincoln
by Ruth Belov Gross
Lothrop, 1990

Share stories about the United States' 16th president, Abraham Lincoln.

Lincoln Memorial Scrapbooks
Have students write and draw pictures about what they have learned in a Lincoln Memorial scrapbook. Enlarge the Lincoln Memorial pattern on page 90. Provide each child with a pattern and construction paper to make covers and pages for their scrapbooks.

All About Abraham Lincoln
by Bruce Knobloch

More Books About the Civil War

A Picture Book of Abraham Lincoln
by David A. Adler, Holiday House, 1989
Anthony Burns: The Defeat and Triumph of a Fugitive Slave
by Virginia Hamilton, Knopf, 1988
Behind Rebel Lines: The Incredible Story of Emma Edmonds
by Seymour Reit, Harcourt Brace Jovanovich, 1988
Behind the Blue and the Gray
by Delia Ray, Lodestar, 1991
The Boy's War
by Jim Murphy, Clarion, 1990
Charley Skedaddle
by Patricia Beatty, Morrow, 1987
Frederick Douglass: The Black Lion
by Patricia McKissack, Childrens Press, 1987
Frederick Douglass and the Fight for Freedom
by Douglas T. Miller, Facts on File, 1988
Go Free or Die: A Story About Harriet Tubman
by Jeri Ferris, Carolrhoda Books, 1988
Honest Abe
by Edith Kunhardt, Greenwillow, 1993

Jayhawker
by Patricia Beatty, Morrow, 1991
Lincoln, in His Own Words
by Milton Meltzer, Harcourt Brace Jovanovich, 1993
Many Thousand Gone
by Virginia Hamilton, Knopf, 1993
Red Cap
by G. Clifton Wisler, Lodestar, 1991
Robert E. Lee
by Manfred Weidhorn, Atheneum, 1988
The Root Cellar
by Janet Louise Swoboda Lunn, Puffin, 1983
Sojourner Truth
by Victoria Ortiz, Lippincott, 1974
War, Terrible War
by Joy Hakim, Oxford University Press, 1993
What Are You Figuring Now? A Story About Benjamin Banneker
by Jeri Ferris, Carolrhoda Books, 1988
Who Comes with Cannons?
by Patricia Beatty, Morrow, 1992

Harriet Tubman

The Age of Invention (1870-1920)
Natural Resources and Immigrant Populations

America experienced its greatest industrial growth after the Civil War. The people believed America had an endless supply of natural resources such as coal, iron ore, and other metals. The government encouraged industrial growth and inventors made it possible for industries to change and grow rapidly. Growing immigrant populations also increased the production of many industries.

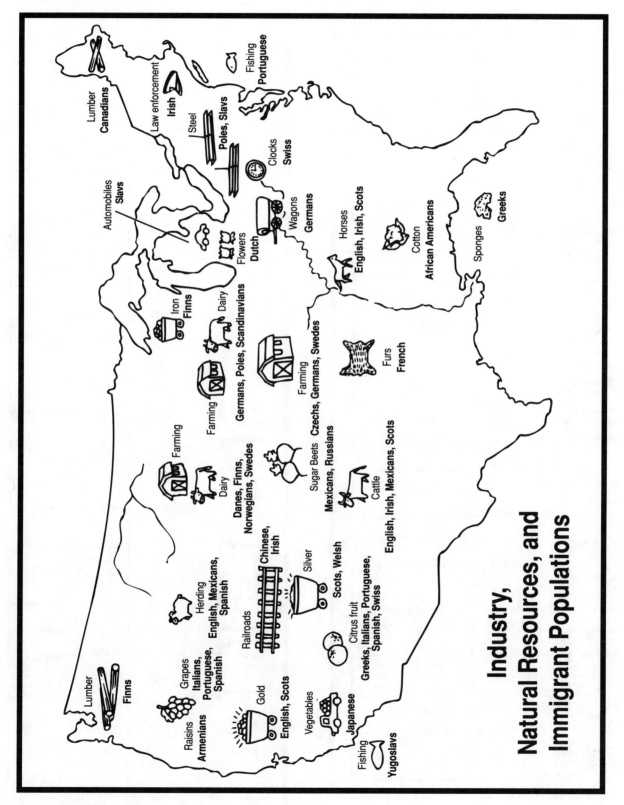

Industry, Natural Resources, and Immigrant Populations

The Age of Invention
Inventions of the Industrial Revolution

Communication, transportation, home life, medicine, science, and military inventions of the late 1800s and early 1900s affected the lives of every American, while the inventions of Thomas Alva Edison, Alexander Graham Bell, and Henry Ford changed the entire world.

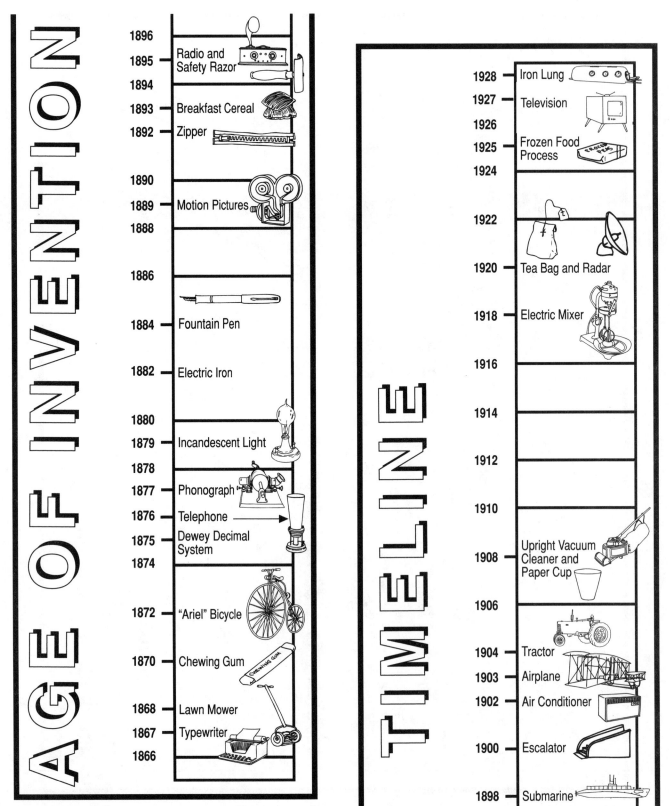

AGE OF INVENTION

- 1896
- 1895 — Radio and Safety Razor
- 1894
- 1893 — Breakfast Cereal
- 1892 — Zipper
- 1890
- 1889 — Motion Pictures
- 1888
- 1886
- 1884 — Fountain Pen
- 1882 — Electric Iron
- 1880
- 1879 — Incandescent Light
- 1878
- 1877 — Phonograph
- 1876 — Telephone
- 1875 — Dewey Decimal System
- 1874
- 1872 — "Ariel" Bicycle
- 1870 — Chewing Gum
- 1868 — Lawn Mower
- 1867 — Typewriter
- 1866

TIMELINE

- 1928 — Iron Lung
- 1927 — Television
- 1926
- 1925 — Frozen Food Process
- 1924
- 1922
- 1920 — Tea Bag and Radar
- 1918 — Electric Mixer
- 1916
- 1914
- 1912
- 1910
- 1908 — Upright Vacuum Cleaner and Paper Cup
- 1906
- 1904 — Tractor
- 1903 — Airplane
- 1902 — Air Conditioner
- 1900 — Escalator
- 1898 — Submarine

Bulletin Board: An Age of Invention Community

1. Enlarge the patterns on pages 96-102.
2. Color and cut out the patterns.
3. Cover your bulletin board with yellow paper.
4. Add an orange bulletin board border.
5. Enlarge, color, and cut out the title below.
6. Arrange and attach the patterns to your bulletin board.

An Age of Invention
Community

Bulletin Board Patterns:
An Age of Invention Dwelling

Dwellings were different in different regions. In some areas, homes looked like giant gingerbread houses with elaborate designs decorating almost every nook and corner.

In large cities, single-family homes were two- or three-story brick structures. Wealthier families even had rooms for their servants.

Bulletin Board Patterns:
Animals of the Age of Invention

There was little change in the animals found during this period of American history. However, certain regions had more of some kinds of animals than others.

For example, horses and a variety of cattle such as Hereford and longhorns were found on cattle ranches in the West. Other regions maintained a variety of farm animals, and city dwellers often kept domestic pets such as dogs and cats.

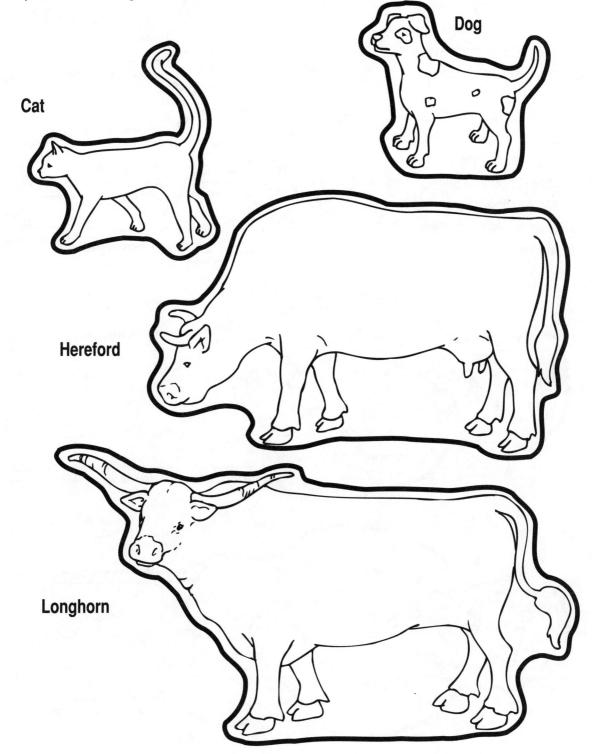

Dog

Cat

Hereford

Longhorn

Bulletin Board Patterns: People of the Age of Invention

Men wore suits similar to formal suits worn today. Grown men wore long pants, starched collar shirts, vests, coats, and hats such as caps or derbies. They wore leather shoes and stockings held up with garters.

Young boys, however, did not wear long pants. They wore knickers, bow ties, and either broad-brimmed hats or caps that matched their outfits.

Clothing changed as more people became interested in sports. Both men's and women's clothing changed to more functional styles that allowed easier movement. Some clothing styles were also influenced by European immigrants.

Bulletin Board Patterns: People of the Age of Invention

Women's dresses changed from floor length to ankle length to calf length during this period. Dress styles included high collars, narrower skirts, bustles, and a variety of decorative satin ribbons, lace, embroidery, and fur trimmings. Hats were worn by most women. Big and small feathered hats were very popular. Young girls wore shorter dresses with stockings, hats, and matching shoes.

Hair styles for women and girls were also different. Women wore their hair up and young girls often wore their hair in ringlets.

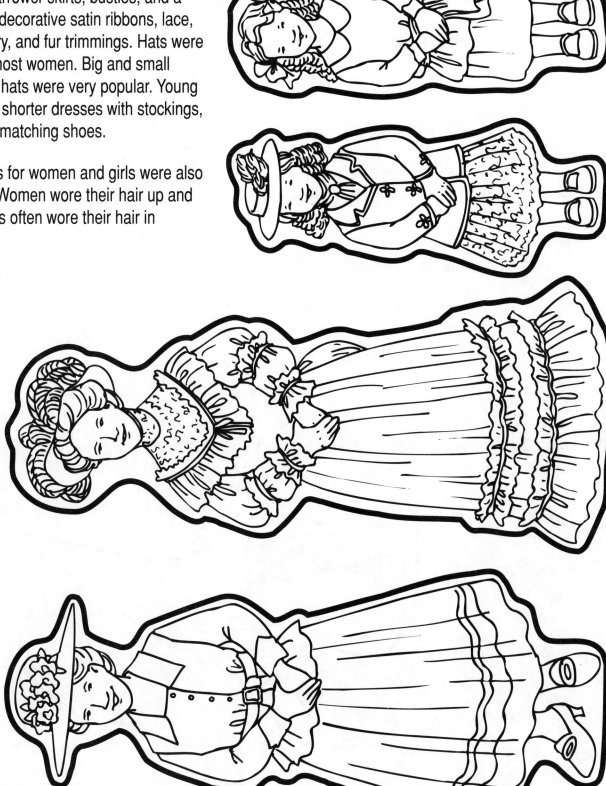

More Patterns for the Age of Invention
Home and Family Life Inventions

Home and family life inventions changed what people wore, how and what they ate, and how they cared for their property and homes.

1. **Lawn mower**, invented in 1868 by Amariah M. Hills.
2. **Incandescent light**, invented in 1879 by Thomas Alva Edison.
3. **Chewing gum**, invented in 1870 by Thomas Adams.
4. **Penny-farthing** or **"Ariel" Bicycle**, invented in 1872 by James K. Starley and William Hillman.
5. **Zipper**, invented in 1892 by Whitcomb L. Judson.
6. **Safety razor**, invented in 1895 by King C. Gillette.
7. **Air conditioner**, invented in 1902 by Willis H. Carrier.
8. **Upright vacuum cleaner**, invented in 1908 by J. Murray Spangler.
9. **Electric food-mixer**, invented in 1918 by the Universal Company.
10. **Shredded Wheat**, a breakfast cereal, invented in 1893 by Henry D. Perky.
11. **Tea bag**, invented in 1920 by Joseph Krieger.
12. **Dewey Decimal System**, library cataloguing, invented in 1875 by Melvil Dewey.

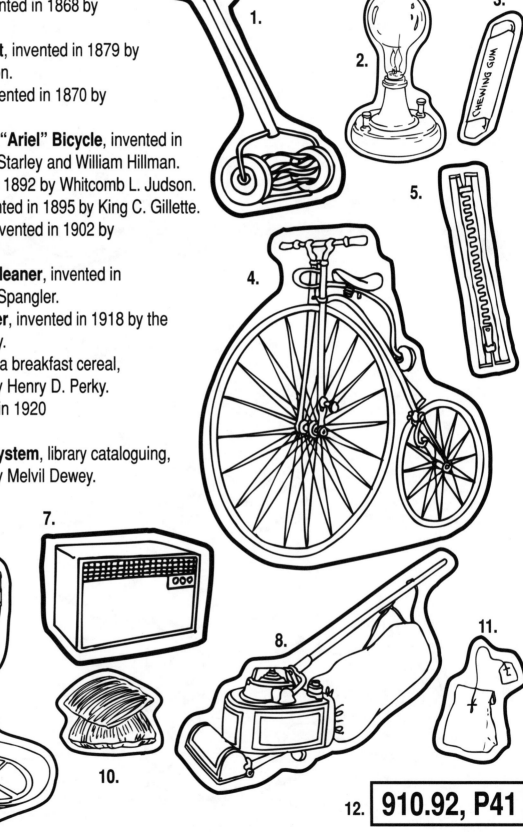

12. 910.92, P41

More Patterns for the Age of Invention
Communication and Transportation Inventions

Communication and transportation inventions changed the world.

1. **Typewriter**, invented in 1867 by Christopher L. Sholes and others.
2. **Telephone**, invented in 1876 by Alexander Graham Bell.
3. **Radio**, invented and modified between 1895 and 1902 by Guglielmo Marconi, Reginald Fessenden, and others.
4. **Phonograph**, invented in 1877 by Thomas Alva Edison.
5. **Television**, invented and modified between 1884 and 1930 by Philo Farnsworth and others. The first electronic transmission occured in 1927.
6. **Fountain pen**, invented in 1884 by Louis E. Waterman.
7. **Paper cup** for drinking, invented in 1908 by the Public Cup Vendor Company.
8. **Motion pictures**, invented and modified between 1889 and 1896 by Thomas Alva Edison, Charles Francis Jenkins, and others.
9. **Airplane**, invented in 1903 by Orville and Wilbur Wright.

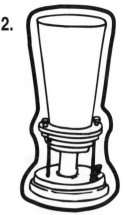

1.

2.

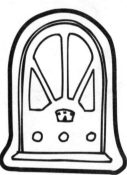

3. 1920s

3. 1930s

4.

4.

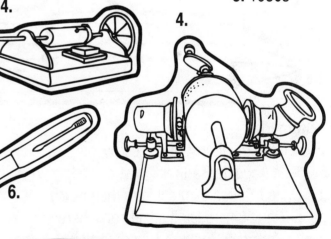

5.

6.

7.

8.

9.

More Patterns for the Age of Invention
Other Inventions and Landmarks

1. **Tractor**, invented in 1904 by Benjamin Holt.
2. **Iron lung**, invented in 1928 by Philip Drinker and Louis A. Shaw.
3. **Modern submarine**, invented in 1898 by John. P. Holland.
4. **Escalator**, invented in 1900 by the Otis Elevator Company.

1.

2.

3.

Statue of Liberty

Landmark

The Statue of Liberty, designed by Frédéric Auguste Bartholdi, was given to the United States as a gift from the French people in 1884. Today it stands on Liberty Island (formerly Bedloe's Island) in New York Harbor. This large copper statue measures over 150 feet high and weighs more than 400,000 pounds.

4.

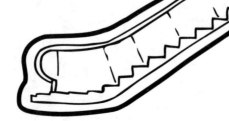

Age of Invention Craft Activities

Let's Make an Age of Invention Diorama

Ask each student to bring an empty shoe box to school. Provide paint and brushes for students to paint their boxes to resemble an Age of Invention community.

Reproduce the patterns on pages 96-102 for students to color, cut out, and glue inside their dioramas.

When dioramas are completed, display student projects on a table in front of your Age of Invention Community bulletin board.

Let's Make a Statue of Liberty Headdress and Torch

Provide each child with 12 triangles, a 2" x 12" oaktag strip, markers, and glue. Instruct children to color one side of the oaktag strip, then have each child wrap and secure the strip to fit his or her head. Show students how to glue the triangles around the headband as shown to form a Statue of Liberty headdress.

Then enlarge and provide each child with a torch pattern to color and cut out.

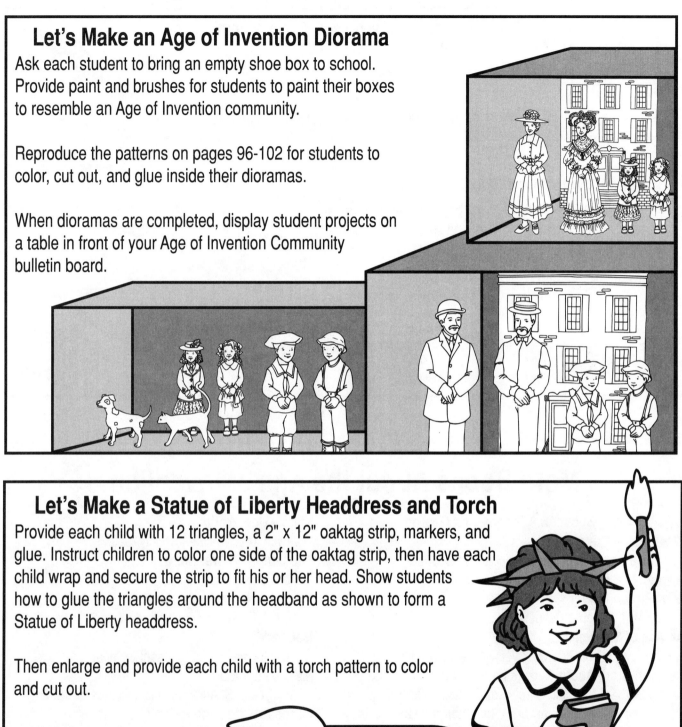

Glue

Age of Invention Literature Links

Guess Again: More Weird and Wacky Inventions
by Jim Murphy
Childrens Press, 1989

Share this book of 45 unusual inventions with your students to inspire ideas for new inventions.

Wild and Wacky Inventions

Provide a variety of craft supplies from the list below, then invite children to design and assemble models of their inventions to share with the class.

cardboard boxes	plastic containers	lids
buttons	corrugated board	poster board
pipe cleaners	plastic straws	paper towel rolls
tissue rolls	markers	scissors
glue	aluminum foil	plastic wrap
thread spools	tape	paint
brushes	paper clips	yarn

Jason's Bow Tying Machine

More Books About the Age of Invention

A Pocketful of Goobers: A Story About George Washington Carver
by Barbara Mitchell, Carolrhoda Books, 1986

A Weed Is a Flower: The Life of George Washington Carver
by Aliki, Simon & Schuster, 1988

An Age of Extremes
by Joy Hakim, Oxford University Press, 1993

Click!: A Story About George Eastman
by Barbara Mitchell, Carolrhoda Books, 1986

Dreamers & Doers: Inventors Who Changed Our World
by Norman Richards, Atheneum, 1984

Ellis Island
by Leonard Everett Fisher, Holiday House, 1986

Ellis Island
by William Jay Jacobs, Scribner's, 1990

... if Your Name Was Changed at Ellis Island
by Ellen Levine, Scholastic, 1993

Immigrant Kids
by Russell Freedman, Dutton, 1980

Klara's New World
by Jeanette Winter, Knopf, 1992

The Long Way Westward
by Joan Sandin, Harper & Row, 1989

Making a New Home in America
by M. B. Rosenberg, Lothrop, Lee & Shepard, 1986

Meet Addy
by Connie Porter, Pleasant Company, 1993

Meet Samantha
by Susan S. Adler, Pleasant Company, 1986

Reconstruction and Reform
by Joy Hakim, Oxford University Press, 1993

Sam Ellis's Island
by Beatrice Siegel, Four Winds Press, 1985

The Store That Mama Built
by Robert Lehrman, Macmillan, 1992

They Sought a New World
by William Kurelek, Tundra, 1985

We'll Race You, Henry, a Story About Henry Ford
by Barbara Mitchell, Carolrhoda Books, 1986

George Washington Carver

The Radio Years (1920-1950)
Highlights of the Radio Years

America experienced the best and the worst of times between the 1920s and the 1950s. These years can be referred to as the "Radio Years" because the radio was one of the most important forms of communication during that time. News and events that affected the entire nation were broadcast over the radio.

April 1922
President Warren Harding throws out the ball to start the 1922 baseball season. The 1922 baseball World Series was the first to be broadcast over the radio.

May 1927
America listens to Charles Lindbergh's progress as he flies across the Atlantic in the Spirit of St. Louis.

October 24, 1929
The New York Stock Exchange collapses and sends the country into a depression. This day is known as "Black Tuesday."

September 1927
Jack Dempsey and Gene Tunney fight for the boxing Heavyweight Championship.

March 12, 1933
President Roosevelt delivers the first of his addresses to the nation known as the "fireside chats."

December 8, 1941
President Roosevelt asks Congress for a declaration of war. America enters history's biggest war, World War II.

December 7, 1941
Japanese bombers attack Pearl Harbor—
"...a day that will live in infamy."
(Franklin D. Roosevelt)

August 9 and 12, 1945
The United States drops two atomic bombs on Japan.

August 14, 1945
The Japanese surrender.

N B C

Lucky Lindy's Transatlantic Flight

The progress of Charles Lindbergh, "Lucky Lindy," as he made his transatlantic solo flight from New York to Paris, was broadcast to millions of people via radio.

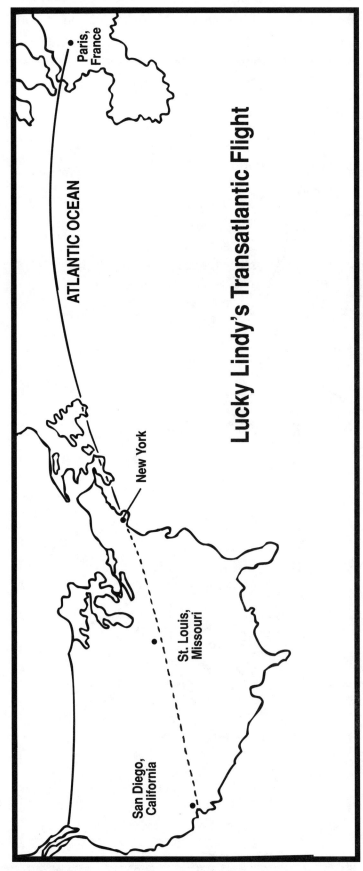

Bulletin Board: A Radio Years Community

1. Enlarge the patterns on pages 108-114.
2. Color and cut out the patterns.
3. Cover your bulletin board with blue paper.
4. Add white clouds and a white bulletin board border.
5. Enlarge, color, and cut out the title below.
6. Arrange and attach the patterns to your bulletin board.

Bulletin Board Patterns: A Radio Years Dwelling

Architecture of the Radio Years was less traditional than it had been. Multifamily apartment buildings were found in many large cities. These structures were designed differently than earlier dwellings. The designs were loose and artistic. One such design style, known as "art deco," can still be seen today in many cities across the nation.

Bulletin Board Patterns:
Animals of a Radio Years Community

Animals found in the United States during the Radio Years were much the same as those found in early America. Animals such as donkeys and horses, once primary forms of transportation, were replaced by the Model T.

The Ford Motor Car Company introduced the Model T in 1924 as practical and stylish transportation.

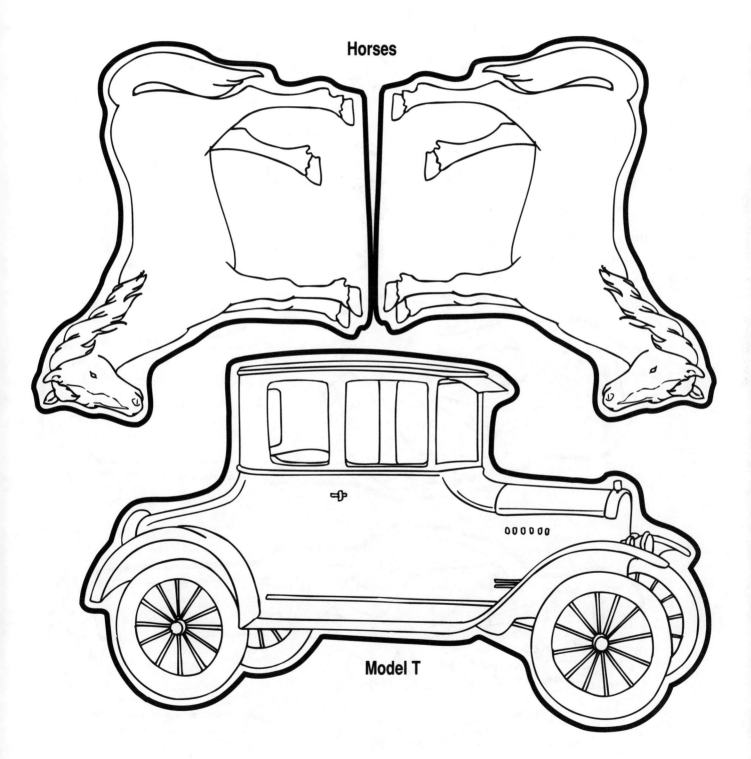

Horses

Model T

Bulletin Board Patterns:
People of a Radio Years Community

During the early Radio Years, people dressed in new yet traditional styles of clothing. As the roles of people changed, so did the styles of the garments they wore. Young people wore fun clothing and new short hair styles.

American and immigrant men wore long, cuffed pants, dress shirts, ties, and coats. Dress coats had wide lapels and pants were often pleated at the waist.

Men also wore hats made of wool felt during the winter months and hats made of straw during the summer months.

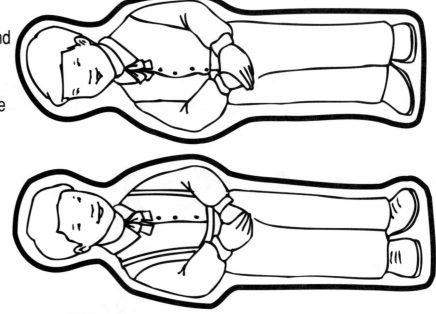

Bulletin Board Patterns:
People of a Radio Years Community

Women's clothing changed dramatically during this time. Dresses went from ankle to calf length.

During the 1920s, young women wore loose-fitting dresses, stockings rolled at the knee, long beaded necklaces, short hair styles, and "cloche," or close-fitting, hats. Some also wore floppy boots. These women were often called "flappers."

Nearing the 1940s, women wore tailored dresses or skirts, blouses, and short jackets with matching berets. Women also began wearing pants more than ever.

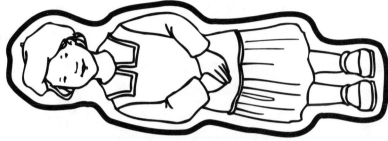

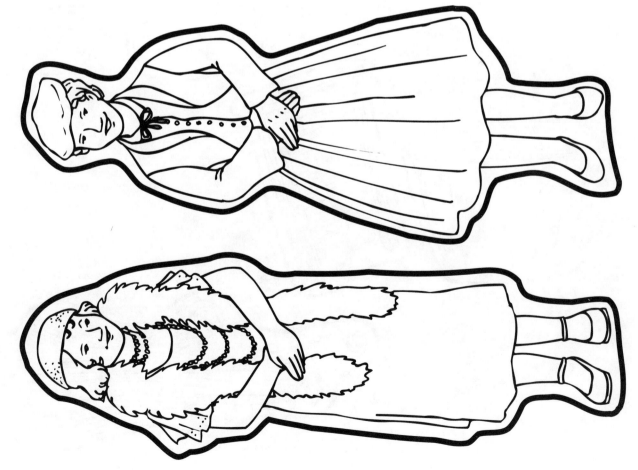

More Patterns for the Radio Years
Food, Utensils, and Industry

Due to the Great Depression, massive unemployment changed the lives of every American. Former millionaires, as well as unemployed workers and their families, stood on soup kitchen lines waiting for food. Every industry was affected by the depression. The few that survived often hired volunteer workers. In large cities like New York, many families lived in shantytowns. They cooked food over open campfires and lived in shack-like structures called shanties.

1. **Kettles** like this held gallons of soup to feed hundreds of unemployed, often homeless people.
2. **Pots** with handles were used instead of bowls to serve soup.
3. **Washboards** were used to hand wash clothing.
4. **Washtubs** were used to wash and carry laundry. They were also used to carry the few belongings families were able to save when they lost all else.
5. **Lumber** was harvested by volunteer forest workers.

More Patterns for the Radio Years
Sports and the War Effort

World War II brought with it new challenges for the people of America. America needed resources to build and make supplies that would help the war effort. Men, women, and children collected tires, scrap metal, and paper toward this effort.

While Americans struggled back to their feet, baseball players such as Ty Cobb and Babe Ruth kept people's minds off their troubles.

1. **Baseball players** became America's heroes.
2. **Tires** provided scrap rubber for the war effort.
3. **Metal utensils** and **old appliances** provided scrap metal for a variety of military supplies.
4. **Newspapers** and other paper scraps were also collected to help the war effort.

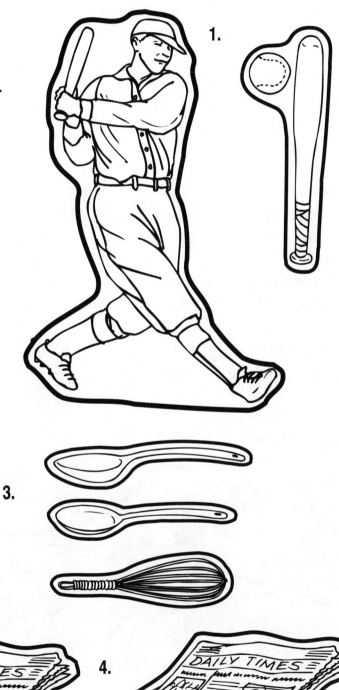

1.

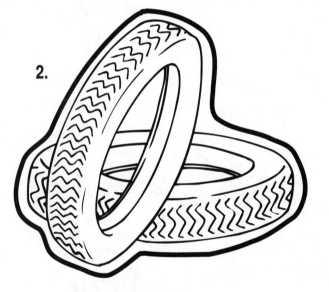

2.

3.

3.

4.

More Patterns for the Radio Years
Toys, Transportation, and Landmark

Most toys were made of either wood or metal. Wooden tops were popular with children of all ages. To spin a top, wrap a string with a loop on one end around the top. Hold the top in the palm of your hand. Place the loop around your middle finger. Then, with a snap of the wrist, release the top with a downward motion. The string unravels and the top should land on the point and spin.

The *Spirit of St. Louis* was the name of Charles Lindbergh's airplane. He flew in it from San Diego, California, to New York before his solo transatlantic flight to Paris, France.

Landmark

Mount Rushmore Memorial, a national monument, honors four American presidents. The heads of George Washington, Thomas Jefferson, Theodore Roosevelt, and Abraham Lincoln were carved from the side of a mountain in South Dakota by Gutzon Borglum in 1927.

Each head measures 60 feet high. The noses are 20 feet long and the eyes are 11 feet wide.

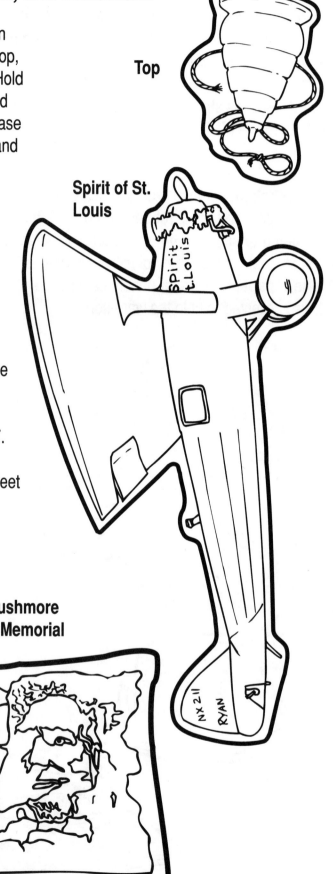

Top

Spirit of St. Louis

Mount Rushmore National Memorial

Radio Years Craft Activities

Let's Make a Radio Years Diorama

Ask each student to bring an empty shoe box to school. Provide paint and brushes for students to paint their boxes to resemble a Radio Years community.

Reproduce the patterns on pages 108-114 for students to color, cut out, and glue inside their dioramas.

When dioramas are completed, display projects on a table in front of your Radio Years Community bulletin board.

Let's Make a Radio Show Booth

Invite students to participate in an oral report activity. Enlarge, color, and cut out the microphone pattern and glue it to a paper towel roll. Cover the bottom and sides of a cardboard box. Fold the top flaps inside and place the box on a table as shown for an interviewer's box. Attach the microphone to the box as shown.

Offer a variety of books about famous Radio Years personalities for children to read. Then provide students with radio cards on which to write information about the famous people. Place the cards in the interviewer's box for the reporter to use during the interviews.

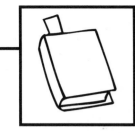

Radio Years Literature Links

Clear the Cow Pasture, I'm Coming in for a Landing!
A Story of Amelia Earhart
by Robert M. Quackenbush
Simon & Schuster, 1990

Learn about the first American woman to fly solo across the Atlantic Ocean.

Let's Make Flight Goggles
Enlarge for each child the pattern that follows and provide scissors, crayons or markers, and yarn to make flight goggles to wear on an imaginary flight. Have children bring knit hats and scarves to wear with their goggles. Encourage children to share their imaginary flight with the class. Ask them to include descriptions of weather conditions, the time of day, their destination, and other factors in their adventure stories.

More Books About the Radio Years

America, I Hear You: A Story About George Gershwin
by Barbara Mitchell, Carolrhoda Books, 1987
An Actor's Life for Me
by Lillian Gish, Viking Kestrel, 1987
Arctic Explorer: The Story of Matthew Henson
by Jeri Ferris, Carolrhoda Books, 1989
Charlie Chaplin
by Gloria Kamen, Atheneum Books, 1982
The Country Artist: A Story About Beatrix Potter
by David R. Collins, Carolrhoda Books, 1989
The Diary of a Young Girl
by Anne Frank, Mooyarart-Doubleday, 1967
The Helen Keller Story
by Catherine Owens Peare, Crowell, 1959
Langston Hughes, American Poet
by Alice Walker, Crowell, 1974
Lost Star
by Patricia Lauber, Scholastic, 1988
Louis Armstrong: An American Success Story
by James Lincoln Collier, Macmillan, 1985

Mary McLeod Bethune
by Eloise Greenfield, Crowell, 1977
Mary McLeod Bethune: A Great American Educator
by Patricia McKissack, Childrens Press, 1985
Meet Molly
by Valerie Tripp, Pleasant Company, 1986
Shirley Temple Black
by James Haskins, Viking Kestrel, 1988
War, Peace, and All That Jazz
by Joy Hakim, Oxford University Press, 1993
Who's That Girl with a Gun? A Story of Annie Oakley
by Robert M. Quackenbush, Prentice-Hall, 1988

Franklin D. Roosevelt

Modern America and the New Frontier (1950-2000)
America's 50 States

By 1959 the New World had grown from a handful of English and Dutch settlements to a nation of 50 states. The United States survived a civil war, two world wars, and the Great Depression. Today, the United States enjoys freedom and continues to fight for freedom for people all over the world.

Modern America and the New Frontier (1950-2000)
America's 50 States

Concord
New Hampshire (9)

Montpelier
Vermont (14)

Augusta
Maine (23)

Lake
Superior

Lake
Huron

St. Paul
Minnesota
(32)

Madison
Wisconsin
(30)

Lansing
Michigan
(26)

Lake Michigan

Lake Erie

Lake Ontario

Albany
New York
(11)

Boston
Massachusetts (6)

Providence
Rhode Island (13)

Des Moines
Iowa (29)

Columbus
Ohio (17)

Harrisburg
Pennsylvania (2)

Hartford
Connecticut (5)

Springfield
Illinois (21)

Indianapolis
Indiana
(19)

Charleston
**West
Virginia**
(35)

Richmond
Virginia (10)

Trenton
New Jersey (3)

Dover
Delaware (1)

Jefferson City
Missouri (24)

Frankfort
Kentucky (15)

Annapolis
Maryland (7)

**Washington, D.C.
(District of Columbia)**

Raleigh
North Carolina (12)

Little Rock
Arkansas (25)

Nashville
Tennessee (16)

Columbia
South Carolina
(8)

Jackson
Mississippi
(20)

Montgomery
Alabama
(22)

Atlanta
Georgia
(4)

Baton Rouge
Louisiana
(18)

Tallahassee
Florida (27)

America's 50 States
Capitals and Order of Admission

Bulletin Board:
A Modern American Community

1. Enlarge the patterns on pages 120-126.
2. Color and cut out the patterns.
3. Cover your bulletin board with blue paper.
4. Add white cutout stars to the background.
5. Add a red bulletin board border.
6. Enlarge, color, and cut out the title below.
7. Arrange and attach the patterns to your bulletin board.

A Modern American
Community

Bulletin Board Patterns: A Modern American Dwelling

Today, Americans from many cultural backgrounds live in single-family dwellings, trailers, condominiums, and modern multifamily apartment complexes. Multifamily structures are built from a variety of materials and often include swimming pools, exercise rooms, and roof gardens.

Bulletin Board Patterns:
Animals of a Modern American Community

Animals found in modern America include a variety of pets. Cats, dogs, and a variety of exotic birds and fish are favorite pets in many families.

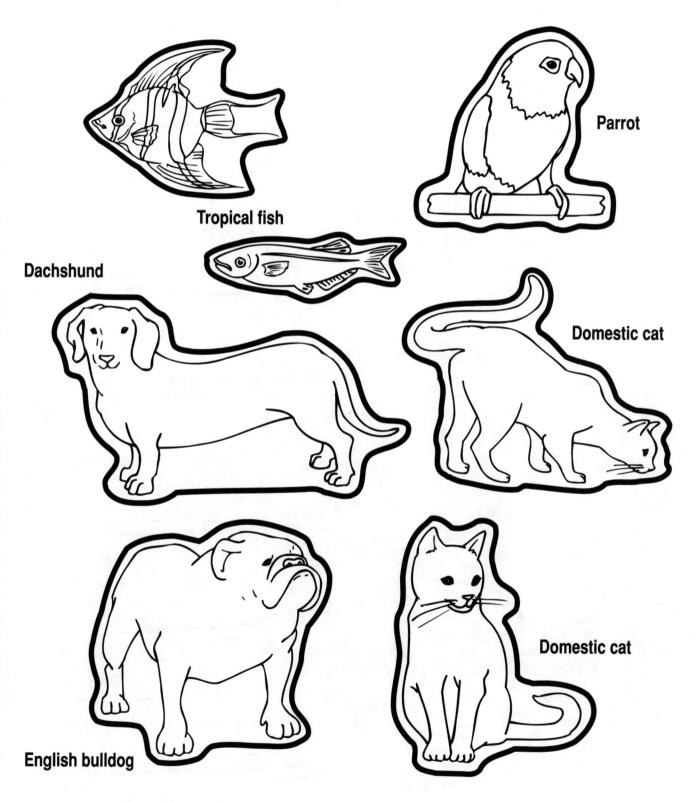

Tropical fish

Parrot

Dachshund

Domestic cat

English bulldog

Domestic cat

Bulletin Board Patterns:
People of a Modern American Community

Both men's and women's clothing styles have changed over the last 200 years. However, some basics still remain.

Men wear traditional-style clothing to formal occasions. More relaxed styles are worn every day. Active sportswear garments have become popular with all Americans.

Garments are made from a variety of natural and synthetic fibers.

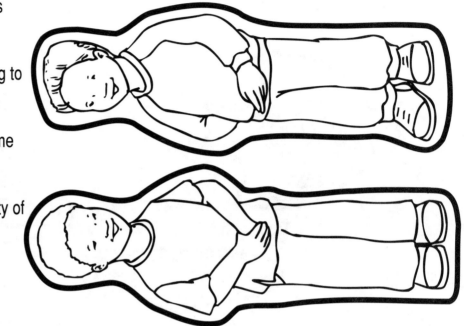

Bulletin Board Patterns:
People of a Modern American Community

Some people wear clothing styles that reflect their cultural heritage. Others continue to design new garments for the future.

Women still wear dresses, skirts, and blouses, or pants and tops.

More Patterns for Modern America
Food and Household Items

Food and cooking appliances changed with new and improved inventions. Foods are packaged in a variety of containers including plastic, paper, metal, and glass. Fast-food restaurants also changed the way people live.

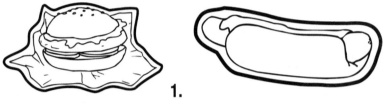

1. **Fast foods** such as hamburgers, hot dogs, and french fries are American favorites.

2. **Microwave ovens**, invented in 1945 by Percy LeBaron Spencer, changed the way Americans prepare foods.

3. **Automatic coffee pots** were first used in 1952. Today at least one can be found in most American homes.

1.

1.

2.

3.

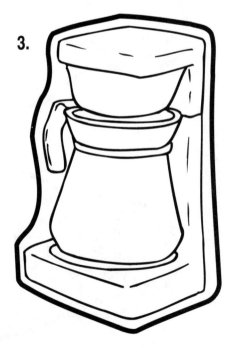

More Patterns for Modern America
Communications and Entertainment

Today, cordless and cellular phones are changing the communications industry. The movie, television, and music industries have also experienced dramatic changes. Movies can be viewed in private homes via VCRs, and families can enjoy the sounds of a grand piano through a portable keyboard.

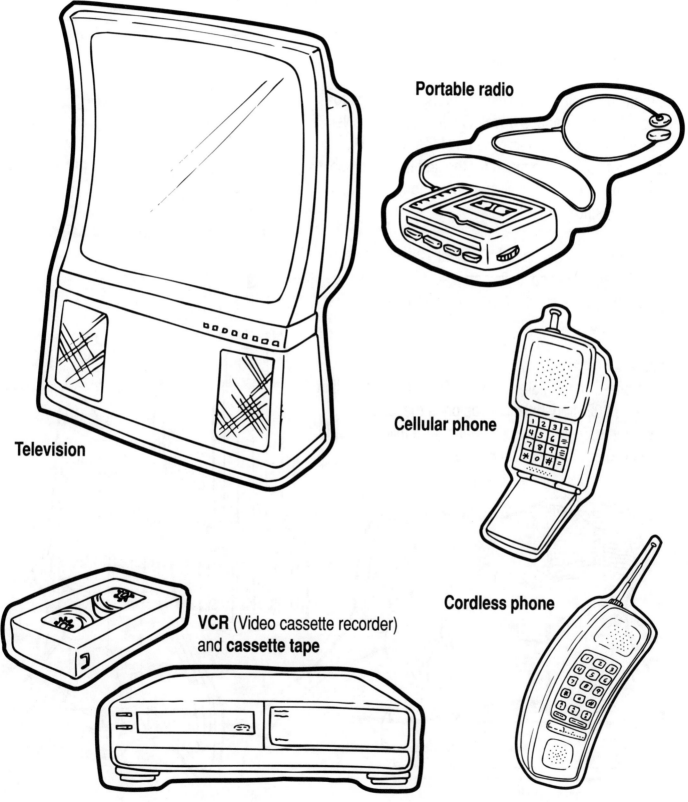

Portable radio

Television

Cellular phone

Cordless phone

VCR (Video cassette recorder) and **cassette tape**

More Patterns for Modern America
Energy, Transportation, Landmark, and the New Frontier

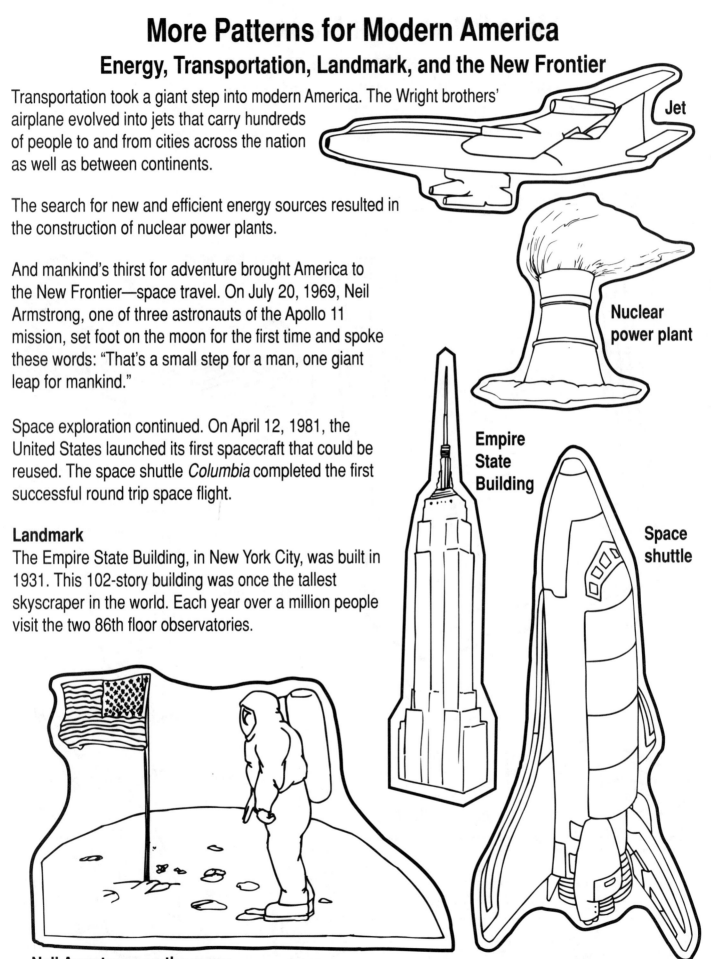

Transportation took a giant step into modern America. The Wright brothers' airplane evolved into jets that carry hundreds of people to and from cities across the nation as well as between continents.

The search for new and efficient energy sources resulted in the construction of nuclear power plants.

And mankind's thirst for adventure brought America to the New Frontier—space travel. On July 20, 1969, Neil Armstrong, one of three astronauts of the Apollo 11 mission, set foot on the moon for the first time and spoke these words: "That's a small step for a man, one giant leap for mankind."

Space exploration continued. On April 12, 1981, the United States launched its first spacecraft that could be reused. The space shuttle *Columbia* completed the first successful round trip space flight.

Landmark

The Empire State Building, in New York City, was built in 1931. This 102-story building was once the tallest skyscraper in the world. Each year over a million people visit the two 86th floor observatories.

Jet

Nuclear power plant

Empire State Building

Space shuttle

Neil Armstrong on the moon

Modern American Craft Activities

Let's Make a Modern American Diorama

Ask each student to bring an empty shoe box to school. Provide paint and brushes for students to paint their boxes to resemble a Modern American community.

Reproduce the patterns on pages 120-126 for students to color, cut out, and glue inside their dioramas.

When dioramas are completed, display student projects on a table in front of your Modern American Community bulletin board.

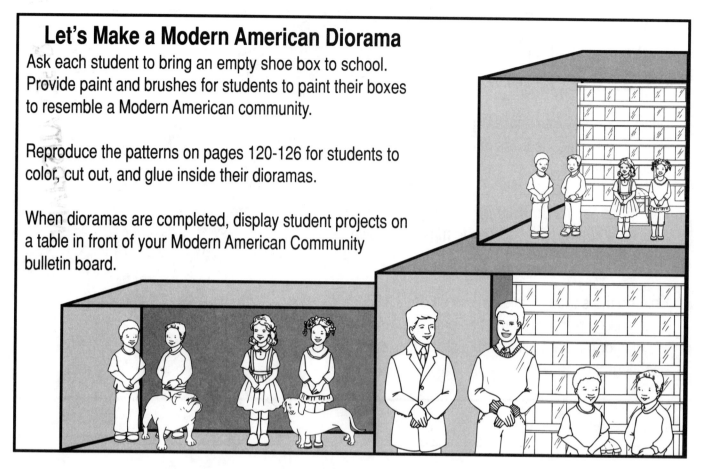

Let's Make an Alien City

Invite children to discuss life forms from outer space after completing a unit on space travel.

Provide students with paper towel and tissue rolls and a variety of craft materials to make Martians and other alien creatures. Then have children paint shoe and tissue boxes to make a city for their extra-terrestrials. Display your alien city on a table in your classroom.

Modern American Literature Links

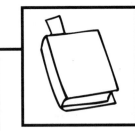

To Space and Back
by Sally Ride
Lothrop, Lee & Shepard, 1986

Share a journey into space with your class and Sally Ride. Then invite the class to participate in a bi-weekly space adventure.

My Space Travel Journal
Provide students with supplies to make their own space travel journals.

Enlarge the space shuttle pattern on page 126 for each child. Provide construction paper, scissors, crayons or markers, glue, and a stapler to assemble each journal.

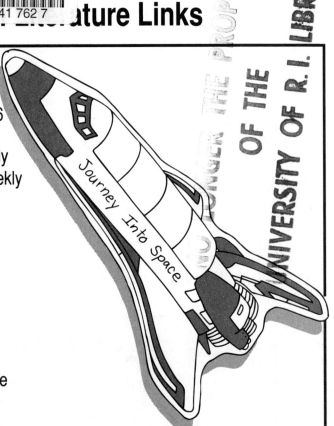

Journey Into Space

More Books About Modern America

All the People
by Joy Hakim, Oxford University Press, 1993

The Astronaut Training Book for Kids
by Kim Long, Lodestar, 1990

Daring the Unknown: A History of NASA
by Howard E. Smith, Harcourt Brace Jovanovich, 1987

The Day We Walked on the Moon
by George Sullivan, Scholastic, 1990

The Dream Is Alive
by Barbara Embury, Harper & Row, 1990

Flying Free
by Philip S. Hart, Lerner, 1992

From Sputnik to Space Shuttles
by Franklyn Mansfield Branley, Crowell, 1986

Get Ready for Robots!
by Patricia Lauber, Crowell, 1988

Living in Space
by Larry Kettlekamp, Morrow, 1993

Power Machines
by Ken Robbins, Holt & Company, 1993

Radical Robots
by George Harrar, Simon & Schuster, 1990

Ramona: Behind the Scenes of a Television Show
by Elaine Scott, Morrow Junior Books, 1988

Robots
by Fredericka Berger, Greenwillow, 1992

Robots: Your High-Tech World
by Gloria Skurzynski, Bradbury Press, 1990

Rockets & Satellites
by Franklyn Mansfield Branley, Crowell, 1987

See Inside a Space Station
by Robin Kerrod, Warwick Press, 1988

Space Camp
by Anne Baird, Morrow, 1992

The Space Shuttle
by George S. Fichter, Watts, 1990

Space Stations
by Gregory Vogt, Watts, 1990

Steve Caney's Kids America
by Steve Caney, Workman, 1978